She threw her mind into the sending...

The water swirled. She heard a voice. She was being called, beckoned. Quickly she scanned the room. No one else could see or hear anything, she was sure of it. But she could feel the water, the vision pulling her.

And she wanted to go. After all, what could be worse than this? What?

A little piece of her mind protested and said, Wait, not this. If you wish to flee, create something of your own, this isn't yours, you don't know what it is. But, she thought, I can't create my own, I've tried. Someone is offering me something and it's my chance to escape. I just have to say yes.

She could feel Coren's hand on her arm.

"No," she heard him say. "No, don't do it!"

"I will," she cried. "I have to!" And with that she threw her mind into the sending, and her body followed.

TRAVEL TO NEW DIMENSIONS
Read

POINT FANTASY

More Minds
by Carol Matas and Perry Nodelman

Princess Nevermore
by Dian Curtis Regan

Shadow of the Red Moon
by Walter Dean Myers

Book of Enchantments
by Patricia C. Wrede

The Enchanted Forest Chronicles
Dealing with Dragons
Searching for Dragons
Calling on Dragons
Talking to Dragons
by Patricia C. Wrede

Of Two Minds

❖❖❖❖❖❖

by Carol Matas
and
Perry Nodelman

SCHOLASTIC INC.
New York Toronto London Auckland Sydney

No part of this publication may be reproduced in whole or in part, or stored in a retrieval system, or transmitted in any form or by any means, electronic, mechanical, photocopying, recording, or otherwise, without written permission of the publisher. For information regarding permission, write to Simon & Schuster Books for Young Readers, Simon & Schuster Children's Publishing Division, 1633 Broadway, 6th Floor, New York, NY 10019.

ISBN 0-590-39468-1

12 11 10 9 8 7 6 5 4 3 2   8 9/9 0 1 2 3/0

Printed in the U.S.A.   01

First Scholastic printing, June 1998

The two authors wish to dedicate this

book to their two families.

Perry's family:

Billie, Josh, Asa, and Alice

Carol's family:

Per, Rebecca, and Sam

1

The castle was quite empty. She knew she was alone, and she liked it that way. It was peaceful.

She looked in the mirror. Not bad, not bad at all.

She had on a white dress, made of gossamer lace. It had a low square neck and was gathered under her breasts, then dropped to the ground with a slight flare at the bottom. The material was light and transparent, so she wore a white satin shift beneath it. Rose pink scarves were tied to the cuff of each puffed translucent sleeve and trailed almost to the ground. Her fine pale hair was tied up on top of her head and interwoven with rose pink ribbon. Her skin was white with a touch of color in the cheeks, her eyes a pale green. Her brow was high and unlined.

She smiled at herself. Her teeth were perfect, even, and white; her lips full, just right for pouting.

She tried a pout. Beautiful.

Now what should she do? She was dressed, she was ready, but for what?

A knight, perhaps. A dark-haired, wildly handsome fellow with a full dark beard who would bow before her and, in a low, passionate voice, tell her how beautiful she was, how tempting, how much he adored her. And then, then, he would leap up from his low bow in an unrestrained fit of passion and sweep her off her feet and—

But no, she didn't want that. Not really. After all, what fun could there be in being swept off your feet, bowled over by someone else's strong will? As if she wasn't pushed around enough already by her own father and mother. And the dress—well, it was pretty, to be sure, but it wasn't very practical. There wasn't much else you could do in a dress like that, except be swept off your feet. She'd try something else, something more adventurous.

She closed her eyes for a moment, then gazed at herself in the mirror again. Now she saw herself in shiny black tights, high-heeled leather boots that reached to midthigh, a short tight purple jacket, and a small black pillbox hat that sat on the middle of her head.

She felt the smooth material of the jacket and grinned. Just like something out of one of her fantasy books, where brave heroines fought battles and saved the world. As she thought of those books, the castle changed around her. The large fireplace, huge upholstered chairs, and stone walls gave way to gleaming white walls and floors, low black stools, and glossy black sofas.

But now what? Aliens to fight, maybe. Slimy green spiderlike creatures with bulging red eyes and tentacles, oozing their way toward her across that gleaming white floor.

As she thought it, still gazing into the mirror, she could see a wispy image of a tentacle begin to materialize behind her, a long slimy tube of horror—

No, she thought, a little frightened. Not that. That's a bit too horrible. And anyway, she told herself, I'd rather think of pleasant things.

A perfect world, maybe. A world where she could have everything the way she wanted it. Now that would be something. She'd make everything beautiful and perfect and interesting—never boring or dull. She'd see to it that everybody was happy, even her parents, whether they liked it or not. She'd make it just the way it ought to be. The way it would be, if only everybody wasn't so stodgy and old-fashioned.

But not today. Today she didn't want perfection. Or excitement, for that matter. It was all so tiring. Today she just wanted to relax, to give in to sheer pleasure and indulge herself.

Perhaps her first impulse was the best, after all. It was a magnificent dress. And all she'd have to do is keep the knight out of it, out of her thoughts.

She returned to the castle and the lovely white dress, and told herself to relax and enjoy it. But as soon as she did relax a little, thoughts of that knight began to enter her head again, and she had to put some effort into keeping him from appearing at her feet. Suddenly, as if produced by her anxiety, a small pink dog appeared, materializing out of the air.

"Oh, how sweet!" she exclaimed aloud. This was much better than the knight. Much safer.

The dog had a round nose, long ears, big eyes, short body, and small stubby legs—it looked very much like a puppy. A harmless puppy, the perfect companion. It barked.

Another dog appeared at its side. This one was blue. Even better. Then another in green. Then purple, red, orange, yellow, brown, gray, black, white. She was very pleased. They were sweet. A gift from an admirer, she thought playfully, something to keep her busy and remind her of him. The pink one jumped up on her dress, just below the waist. The dress tore, the dog clawing its way down.

"Don't," she laughed.

But it did, again, and then it was joined by others. Soon they were all over her, clawing, nipping, biting. Her dress was in tatters. It wasn't fun anymore. She decided to make them go away.

They wouldn't. They wouldn't stop, and they wouldn't go away. She felt a surge of panic. Why couldn't she make them go away? She turned and fled.

She ran to the top of the stairs. The dogs were right behind her. She skipped, taking the steps three at a time, but she wasn't fast enough. The dogs barked and yapped and began to howl.

From where she stood, the staircase went down four floors. She sprang onto the banister and slid down. Why not? The dress was ruined already.

Yes, now she was ahead of them. She reached the first landing, ran around to the top of the next flight, leaped onto the next banister, and slid down again. Her hair tumbled around her. If she could only get out the main door at the bottom and call for help. There would be servants below, gardeners outdoors; someone would be there, had to be there. She willed them to be there.

She could see the bottom now, and at the next landing, she leaned over the banister for a better view. A huge white form blocked the doorway. It was a massive white bear, very round, very beautiful, really. But she knew she would never get past it.

And she didn't know where it had come from, couldn't imagine where it had come from. That was the scariest part.

What could she do now? Ah-ha, she had it! Her own room could be on the floor she was on right now. Yes, her own room was there, just down the corridor, and there were instructions pasted up on the wall, what to do in case of emergency.

She hurried down the hall and was relieved to find that the room was there, just as she'd imagined it. She ran past the huge curtained bed and quickly began reading the instructions. No, not that one, that was for magicians, another for bad people, useless, ah, there it was, dogs. A recipe for dog trouble.

And she had to use it fast; they were on her trail now. She could see the pink one dart into the room. It barked, a sharp happy bark. She was trapped. She was theirs.

Turn three times, she was reading so fast, she hoped it was right, saying in a low voice, "Dominic, Dominic, Dominic."

She did so. Her scarves waved gracefully around her as she turned and turned and said low, "Dominic, Dominic, Dominic." The dogs were now huge bears. In front of them appeared a knight, dressed in armor, ten others with him, swords ready for battle. In unison they said, "At it, at it, at it," as they struck down the animals.

When all was quiet, the main knight removed his helmet and approached her. He was dark-haired and wildly handsome, with a square jaw and smoldering eyes.

"Thank you, kind sir," she said to him, holding out her hand.

He shrugged and replied, "I'm rather good at my job." And he leaned over to kiss her hand.

"Your—uh—Your Highness?"

The timid voice came from behind her, but Lenora

knew it belonged to Sylvie, her mother's maid. And suddenly the knight was gone, and the castle too, and she was back in her real room. The mirror reflected just a simple blue shift reaching to the knees, white sandals, long straight blond hair falling loosely around a blue hair band and framing a face that was, well, quite lovely, certainly—but surrounded by all this mediocrity, what did it matter?

So dreary, Lenora thought, gazing at her reflection. So dull.

The room was plain, too. Pale pink walls, a four-poster bed, a small couch covered in a blue and white pattern, a fireplace, mahogany chests of drawers and wardrobe. Solid, handsome, practical, dull. Dull, dull, dull.

"Well, Sylvie," she sighed, not even bothering to turn around, "what is it?"

"Your Highness, your mother wishes to see you in her apartment." Sylvie paused, then cleared her throat. "Uh—and she told me to tell you that she means now, right now."

Right now indeed. For a brief instant, Lenora wondered if she hadn't been better off with the dogs and the bears.

2

Just as she thought—her mother was steaming.

"I'll have you know, Lenora, that we've all been hanging around in the middle of nowhere, in some awful gray place, doing nothing for I don't know how long! And it was your fault, I know it was. You've obviously defied my orders and imagined some silly world of your own again—and as usual, of course, it has to be a world where your dear, sweet mother doesn't even exist. And right in the middle of my busiest time of the day, too! A dinner menu to plan, towels to sort, housecleaning to supervise, and poof!—the house is suddenly gone, and there I am, hanging around in that awful gray nothingness, for what seemed to be forever! It was you, wasn't it? I know it was you, Lenora, it always is. Just what silly thing did you make up this time?"

Lenora tried to think of something harmless to tell her—she certainly didn't want her mother to know the truth, especially about those nasty little dogs.

But Queen Savet didn't wait for an answer. "Never mind," she said, "I don't really care. It was bound to be some childish fantasy or other. Some ridiculous romantic nonsense about dragons, or about knights that adore you like puppies. I know you, Lenora—you and your endless fantasy books."

Lenora blushed.

"And," her mother continued, getting angrier as she went on, "whatever it was, it wasn't important enough to send me and everyone else in the house off into oblivion. This is it! I put my foot down. Never again. Do you understand me? Never again!"

"Yes, Mother," Lenora pouted, kicking at the carpet and hoping that would be all.

But she knew it wouldn't be. When Queen Savet got started on this topic it was almost impossible to stop her—it was like a rock rolling down a mountain.

"Oh yes," said Queen Savet, "you've been an impetuous child from the day you were born. I took one look at you, and I knew. And I told your father, right then, just ask him and see if I didn't. 'Rayden,' I said, 'you mark my words.' And I was right, too! The places I've been! The things you've turned us all into! It's amazing we're still here at all, young lady, and still in one piece."

Blah, blah, blah, thought Lenora. Next it would be the talking chairs.

"Like that awful time when we had the harvest festival," her mother continued. "I'll never forget that, never. Important visitors from ten different countries, and you had to make all the chairs in the banquet hall talk! Talking chairs, of all things, telling everyone how they felt about being sat upon—even poor old Prince Hagupt, of all people. And for those who had the misfortune to be slightly overweight—well, to have a chair inform you of that fact is demeaning, to say the least!"

It isn't fair, Lenora thought. Will I never be allowed to forget that? After all, I was only five years old! And anyway, everyone always took the chairs for granted, just like they always take everything else in the whole stupid world for granted.

And she could still remember all the wonderful confusion. Old Prince Hagupt had turned beet red and stormed out of the room, the pompous fool.

"And then," her mother, of course, continued, "making all the farm animals into stuffed toys that time—you were seven then, weren't you? There was nothing to eat for a week but oatmeal porridge. I hate porridge!"

So do I, thought Lenora—but I made mine taste like roast beef. Why didn't you? Why didn't anybody in this whole stupid country ever use their gift for anything interesting? What was the point of being able to make whatever you imagine real if you never actually did it?

Well, Lenora sighed, her mother was about to tell her. Again. For a brief instant, she considered turning her mother into a frog. A slimy green frog, with a sock in its mouth to stop it from croaking on and on and on. But that would get her into even worse trouble. Better just listen and get it over with.

"Oh, Lenora, Lenora," Queen Savet wailed, "you've studied your history. You know your politics. You know the struggles our ancestors had to go through before they finally figured out how to deal with our gift—the battles, the chaos. You know they thought long and hard about the best world for us Gepethians to live in, once they finally agreed to work together as a team. And once they created that world—this world, Lenora, the one we all share—they made a promise to keep it as it was until everyone agreed to change it—everyone, acting together. And we all still honor that promise, as you well know."

Nobody ever consulted me about it, Lenora thought. She contented herself with just imagining the sock in her mind, its woolly end sticking out of the corner of her mother's mouth. It wasn't nearly as satisfying as actually making it happen.

And it certainly didn't stop the flow of words. "It's a good world, too," her mother continued, "a good, balanced world. A place for everything, and everything in its place. Why can't you just accept it, like everybody else in Gepeth?"

Queen Savet paused, as if actually waiting for an answer. Lenora blinked the sock in her mind out of existence and tried to think of the right answer.

Because it's boring, she thought. Boring boring boring. "I don't know," she finally mumbled.

But her mother didn't hear her. "And even if it weren't a good world, then we'd change it by consensus, by agreement. Nobody would get to force their world on anybody else. Your father may be a king, Lenora, but he isn't a dictator, no matter what you think. No, Rayden can't just impose his will on others, Lenora, and neither can you. You can't. We've told you that again and again, Lenora, again and again and again! And yet there I was in that gray nothing for hours, and the towels not even folded!"

"I'm sorry, Mother." And she really was, too. It had been a stupid thing to do. If she hadn't gotten carried away by that knight, she would have made sure everyone else had kept on existing somewhere else—in some parallel world, maybe, where there were mountains of towels in need of folding and her mother would think she'd died and gone to heaven.

But then Lenora had another thought. "But Mother, if you didn't like me sending you off like that," she asked, "then why did you allow it? You have the gift, too. Couldn't you have just imagined yourselves back here, and then you would have been here? Why did it happen that way?"

"I don't know," Queen Savet grumbled. "I just don't know. I tried, I certainly did try—when those towels will get done I can't imagine. You have more power than is good for anyone, Lenora, and well, frankly, I tried and I couldn't do anything. You seem to be getting stronger day by day. If your father hadn't been away, perhaps . . ." Her mother looked at Lenora questioningly, as if she weren't altogether certain about that.

"At any rate," her mother continued, "it'll soon be over, thank goodness. On your seventeenth birthday you'll be married, and all this nonsense will be over. Your husband will make sure of that."

Her husband indeed. She'd like to see him try.

But her mother went on and on, and her words still echoed in Lenora's head as she slammed the front door of the house behind her and stamped down the path, furious. How often would she have to listen to that lecture? If she had to sit through it one more time she would go absolutely insane.

Lenora stopped for a moment on the path, trying to shake off her anger at her mother, thinking about where to go.

Lufa. She would visit Lufa. She was the only person Lenora could talk to. All the other adults were just like her mother, and as for people her own age, forget it—they were all such cowards. Such good little Gepethians, never even changing the color of their hair.

And anyway, she was rarely allowed contact with

them. She was royalty after all, and as Queen Savet and King Rayden were constantly telling her, she couldn't fraternize with just anyone. And yet everyone blindly agreed to it. What a stupid system!

The cobblestone pavement jarred Lenora's slim frame as she headed off toward Lufa's cottage through the winding streets of the village, angrily muttering to herself.

And I won't marry! she told herself. They can't make me. Marry! So I can do nothing but sew, and make menus, and waste my time with all that useless practical stuff! Why on earth did they decide on a world like this one, with so much boring work in it? Why not one with machines that do everything for you? I mean, here we are, using candles when we could just flip a switch and have light, like they do in fantasy books! Or have machines to drive us, instead of horses. Or we could even fly in the air! But no, not us, we have to leave things as they are just because the old fogies think it's better that way; we have to always worry about keeping the balance. The stupid balance. I hate the balance!

And anyway, she went on to herself, it's just because they can't imagine anything better. They're too old and tired to think up anything interesting anymore. Or even if they can, they don't have the courage to do anything except write about it. They put it in books, and they're happy just to sit around all day reading about different ways of life instead of actually experiencing them. What cowards.

Well, she murmured as she stalked up to Lufa's cottage, that's not enough for me. And I won't be bullied into it!

Lufa's door opened, just as Lenora had her hand up to knock.

"Why Lenora, how nice. I was expecting you. In fact," Lufa said, her musical laugh floating through the air, "I could feel you coming. Like one feels a storm cloud approaching."

Lenora let out a small giggle.

"Only they make me so mad."

"Yes dear," said Lufa, "I know."

Lenora wasn't sure just how old Lufa was. Perhaps her mother's age, but she was so different from her mother. She had an oval face with olive skin, dark hair cut into a bob, and large brown eyes. She was the medicine woman of the village, and she had a kindly word for everyone.

"I'm going to pick herbs in my garden," Lufa said. "Come along."

Lenora was grateful for the invitation. It would keep her mind occupied. Her feelings of restlessness seemed to be growing by the second, and, well, to be truthful, she was becoming fearful of creating another reality. It wasn't her mother's anger she minded, not really. She was used to that. No, it was losing control that bothered her. Those dogs turning on her—and then, the bears. She was sure she hadn't thought up those bears. Why had it gone wrong like that? What had happened? If her father had been home—well, maybe Lufa could help her figure it out.

Lufa's garden was on the rising slope behind her cottage. It was really more like a small wood, cultivated with special herbs and plants, which eventually joined into the large forest that bordered the north end of the village. It was a restful place, and Lenora felt herself calming down as she helped Lufa and basked in the pleasantly warm morning sun.

For almost an hour they worked in silence, Lufa cutting the herbs and leaves she needed, Lenora holding the wicker basket for her. Finally Lufa paused and picked up the flask of water, which was also in the basket. After taking a swig, she handed it to Lenora. By now the sun was at its peak, and Lenora was starting to feel its strength as it beat down on her head out of a cloudless blue sky. The cool water tasted wonderful.

Lufa gazed at Lenora with concern as she drank. "What happened today?" she asked finally.

"I'm not sure," Lenora replied, taking another gulp from the flask. "I—well, I created something. I know, I know I'm not supposed to, but I just couldn't help it. Lufa, I just couldn't. I was so bored. I imagined something out of one of my books, a perfectly harmless world. But then—well, it kind of took over, like in a dream, and I was in real trouble for a while. I couldn't control it. I imagined some instructions for getting out of it, finally. That was smart of me, wasn't it?" she asked anxiously.

Lufa nodded.

"But even so . . ." Lenora stopped, unsure of how to continue.

"But even so it scared you."

"Well . . ." Lenora didn't exactly want to admit that she had been frightened, even if she had every reason to be. Those dogs and that bear were just as real as she and Lufa were, after all. And so were their claws and their teeth. She could still hear the sound of her dress ripping.

"But how can my own creation hurt me?" Lenora protested. "I mean, if it got dangerous, I'd always be able to create something that would save me, wouldn't I? Like I did today?"

Lufa looked at her thoughtfully.

"I don't know, Lenora," she finally said. "I'm not so sure of that. Your strength is growing by leaps and bounds. The worlds you create are more real all the time. It all comes down to yourself. Whether you realize it or not, all the things you create come from somewhere in your mind."

Lenora was about to protest.

"Of course," Lufa continued, "sometimes it's a place you don't know about, a dark place you've hidden from yourself. And those places are the most dangerous, I think. If you let what's in them loose, you might well not be able to control it. That's why we've all agreed to keep the balance.

"Oh, I know how you feel about the balance, Lenora," Lufa added as she noticed the dismayed look on Lenora's face. "But you're not the only one who feels that way. This questioning, this experimenting is a stage a lot of us Gepethians go through, when we're young. Why, when your own mother was your age, she once—" Lufa suddenly stopped in midsentence.

But she hadn't stopped soon enough. Lenora was astonished. Queen Savet, of all people, fooling around with the balance? And then, having the nerve to give her that lecture! What hypocrisy!

"What did she do?" Lenora demanded.

Lufa colored and turned away. "Never mind," she said. "It's not important. I only mean that you're not the only one who ever skirted the balance a little, that's all. But if you're going to keep on doing it—as I'm sure you are, Lenora—then you have to learn to be more careful. Things might happen—serious things. Perhaps you and I should work together. With me there to teach you control, you might learn to overcome the danger."

Lenora was shocked. She'd expected Lufa to reassure her, not to respond like this. How could her own fantasies be so dangerous? For a moment, an image of that slimy tentacle passed through her mind, and she quickly blotted it out. How could she have things like that hidden inside her? She didn't want to think about it.

"Why don't you sit over there by the fountain," Lufa suggested, noticing Lenora's distress. "It's cool and shady. I have a special plant to tend, and you look tired. I'll be back in a few minutes, and we'll decide what to do."

Thankfully, Lenora headed for the fountain. She was tired, and hot, and confused. She sank down on a stone bench underneath a huge elm. The cold stone bit into her bare legs, making her gasp. For a brief instant, she considered imagining it warmer, and then hesitated, and left it the way it was.

She sat and stared at the pool. There was a little fountain in its center, a stone figure of a wolf standing on its hind legs, spewing rainbow droplets into the air. Small splashes in the pool hinted at the presence of fish. Lenora got up to take a closer look.

She gazed into the water. It rippled. And then she noticed a young man reflected in the pool, just behind her. A stranger.

She whirled around. There was no one there.

She turned in confusion and looked into the pool again. There he was, standing just behind her own image—hair an unruly carrot red, eyes grayish blue, skin white with freckles. He looked a little like a clown, but his high cheekbones and full mouth, which turned up into a slight smile, made him seem almost handsome. Interesting, certainly. Again she turned around, as fast as she could.

No one.

She turned back to the pool, and this time she felt something drawing her. The boy was still there, his reflection rippling behind hers, but something else was there as well, in the pool, in the water. A force, beckoning her, compelling her toward it. Somehow she knew it wasn't the boy producing the feeling. He looked far too terrified, now, for it to be him. No, it was something else. She began to concentrate on it. That force wanted her, needed her. She needed it.

And then she was no longer looking into the pool.

She was standing high on a mountain, looking out over a vast plain. The white spires of a magnificent city gleamed in the distance.

Then the scene shifted. She was in a large group of people, and they were screaming a name, a name she couldn't quite catch. And now they were cheering, wild with joy, and she was cheering with them. She was happy, happier than she had ever been, and she felt something she'd never experienced before. It was a feeling of pure power. She could create, she could destroy at will. She flew over a world, crushing cities, throwing them away like so much garbage. She loved the sensation, reveled in it, rejoiced.

Suddenly she was once again staring into an ordinary pool of water—and immediately she became terrified by the feelings she had so enjoyed a moment before.

Lufa was crouched in front of her, her fingertips resting on Lenora's temple.

"Lenora," she said anxiously. "What is it? What happened?"

3

Prince Coren stood in the middle of a forest, far from home, staring distastefully at his reflection in a mirror propped against the branch of a tree. He hated everything he saw there: the thin frame, the ridiculously pale white skin, the freckles. And worst of all, the hair, the flaming carrot-red hair. He looked like a clown.

Some prize for the poor girl he was traveling to meet. Depressed at how little he resembled the sort of handsome knight in shining armor a princess would expect, he angrily tossed the soapy razor in his hand onto the leaf-strewn ground.

Why had his mother asked King Rayden to give him the stupid razor? Just because they were almost there in Gepeth, in that girl's country, his mother all of a sudden started worrying about the way he looked, of all things. As if anybody in his family ever cared about how they actually looked, instead of just thinking themselves into a different appearance in their own minds. As if he could actually do anything about those freckles, that hair. As if it would make any difference.

And the worst of it was, he didn't have one hair on his face worth shaving.

She'll hate me, he told his image in the mirror. He shook his head in dismay, sending bits of foam flying from his cheeks, and vigorously toweled off the rest of the soap.

The truth was, the closer he got to that girl, the more frightened he was of meeting her.

He'd agreed with his parents, Coren reminded himself, that this marriage between him and King Rayden's daughter seemed ideal. In fact, he'd been even more convinced than they were—for he'd caught a little worrying thought of his mother's about the wisdom of mixed marriages. It seemed that the girl's people were afflicted with an unfortunate congenital handicap and were incapable of reading thoughts as all his countrymen could, as all normal people could—as he could himself.

Well, that was just fine by Coren. In fact, it was the main reason he'd accepted the idea of marrying in the first place. He hated the life of the mind and wanted nothing more than reality, pure and simple.

Yes, a simple, straightforward life, that's all he asked for. One where people couldn't jump into your head uninvited, or where you didn't jump into their heads uninvited. Coren himself had a policy about that, a personal commitment not to listen in on others—not even the animals or insects or all the other living things whose mental energies buzzed continually through the minds of all Andillans. It was hard, but he had decided not to eavesdrop, and he stuck by it, and he was proud of it.

What he wanted was a place where the world was real and solid, not some imagined place that existed only in your head. His parents might be content with the magnificent rooms and mansions they imagined they were living in, inside their minds. But Coren himself was just too sensible to blithely ignore the real dust and ruins that he saw all around him in Andilla, the once beautiful buildings that had been abandoned when people decided that mental dwellings were better than real ones and mental beds softer than real mattresses. In Andilla, it was either imagine a soft place to sleep or else lie on the cold real ground and suffer—as Coren insisted on doing. Gepeth sounded like a paradise in comparison to Andilla.

Of course, Coren was a little frightened when he'd learned that Gepethians could actually change the world they lived in, simply by making whatever they imagined materialize—changing it in your thoughts was more than bad enough, thank you. But he was reassured when his mother reported that the people of Gepeth had all agreed on one world and stuck to it. A world with real beds in it, he hoped— soft ones.

"A pretty boring kind of world it is, too, if you ask

me," his mother had added. "No dragons or anything interesting."

But that was sensible. Dragons were scary, even when you knew they were just in your thoughts. The Gepethians sounded like his kind of people.

Even so, as soon as news of that girl had come into his life, everything had changed, and if there was one thing Coren was sure he didn't like, it was change. It wasn't the princess's fault, of course, but Coren had begun to think that maybe it would have been better just to leave things as they were and to forget about the marriage. It was making everything so complicated and so annoying.

To begin with, as soon as King Rayden had arrived in Andilla with the marriage proposal, there had to be bargaining, endless dealing and negotiating. And, of course, his parents insisted Coren be in on all of it. People were passing back and forth through his mind as if it were the main market square in the village. He was hardly ever left alone anymore, and he hated it.

When he was left alone, it was even worse, because whenever he was by himself, strange ideas and visions had begun to pop into his head, uncontrollably. He'd never had peculiar thoughts like that before, never. Ugly white rooms filled with uncomfortable-looking black furniture. Huge white bears with long dangerous-looking claws. Slimy, tentacled, spiderlike creatures that only some maniac could have imagined.

And dogs—puppies with round noses, long ears, big eyes, short bodies, and stubby legs—silly-looking puppies in different colors, pink, blue, purple, red, orange, yellow, jumping and clawing. Coren began to think that he might be going crazy. And he resolved never to tell her about it, once he met her—she'd really think he was beneath her then, having thoughts like that. She'd probably suppose he had some kind of illness.

Maybe he did. Or, he thought, maybe my mind is warning me off, telling me I'm doing the wrong thing. Why can't I just confront my parents and say no to this marriage? It isn't too late. They claim to love me, don't they? They'll understand and respect my feelings. I'll do it now. I'll walk right up to them and demand to go home. I'll—

Who was he kidding? He'd do no such thing. He was a coward, a disgusting coward. He was doomed. Doomed.

As if in response to his desolation, the mirror fogged over. He put his hand out to clear it, wiping at the moisture on the glass. There was no moisture.

And yet the mirror remained fogged. He put his whole forearm against the mirror so he could rub it clean with his arm. He couldn't. It was as if he were looking at it with his eyes closed.

Coren stood back a little and stared. Now what-was happening? He rubbed the mirror wildly with both hands, at the same time willing his image to return.

But it didn't. Instead, the mirror began to shimmer, and suddenly he saw a beautiful, no, a stunning face— the face of a magnificent young woman with fair hair and blue eyes, her full lips in a sensuous pout. She was wearing a white dress, made of gossamer lace over white satin, with pink scarves trailing from the cuffs of the sleeves. She looked like the kind of lady brave knights went into battle for, fought monsters for.

Then the image in the mirror wavered just a little, and changed. It was still her, still recognizably the same girl, but wearing a simple blue outfit. She seemed not quite so perfect, more human somehow. He liked her better this way—she was less imposing, less frightening.

He looked at the girl with pleasure, almost forgetting that her face ought not to be in his mirror. The image seemed to flicker. It was like a reflection, as if the girl were gazing into water of some kind.

Suddenly, she turned away from him and then turned back again and stared piercingly, right into his eyes. Something had surprised her, something behind her. There, behind her shoulder, he could see himself—a reflection of his own white face and freckles, flickering in the water. Coren was puzzled. How could it be there, when he was here, in the forest?

But there was no time to think about that, he realized. There was danger there, in that scene in the mirror. The girl was being pulled, pulled into the pool by some great force she couldn't resist. Coren broke into a sweat. "No! Don't go!" he heard himself shouting.

"Coren! Coren!"

The sharp voice cut through the spell. The vision disappeared. It was his mother, Queen Milda. And for once he was glad she had intruded on his thoughts, because now he was staring into a clear unfogged mirror hung on a tree in a reassuringly solid forest glen. He could feel his heart beating, and his hands were wet.

He turned around to greet his mother. She wasn't there.

"Of course I'm not there," he heard her say inside his head. "Why would I be? You're the one who insists on actually visiting people physically, instead of just doing the sensible thing and entering their thoughts like everybody else. You won't catch me wasting my time with nonsense like that."

A vision of Queen Milda's face grew inside Coren's mind—her graying hair, her high forehead and beaky nose, her aggressive eyes glinting behind her thick, dark-rimmed glasses.

"Honestly, Coren," the voice went on inside his head, "you are one of us, after all, even if you don't like to admit it. It's just not normal for you not to use the mental powers you were born with. Refusing to read other people's thoughts is against nature."

Well, Coren had heard that before, many times. How often was he going to have to listen to this lecture? If he had to go through it one more time he would go insane.

"Oh, I doubt it," said his mother in his mind. "You've got too much common sense. Indeed, you could do with a little less common sense, if you ask me. Anyway, my boy," Queen Milda went on briskly, "that's not why I'm here. I'm here to calm your fears."

Calm his fears? What fears?

"You know perfectly well what I mean, Coren. Your fears about Princess Lenora. Today's the big day. And this horrible journey King Rayden insisted we take will soon be over. This carriage we're in is despicable—I don't believe it's been out of the stable since your great-great-grandparents' day. And the road is so bumpy that I'm having a hard time thinking it smooth. I don't know why we couldn't have just visited Rayden in his mind, like sensible people do. But I suppose we do have to take his handicap into consideration, poor fellow. Anyway, we arrive in Gepeth soon—it's just a short distance farther until we reach the end of these woods. Why, right at this very minute, King Rayden is out there on the road in front of us, galumphing around on that horse of his with his eyes peeled for a first view of the chimneys of Gepeth."

Then her tone changed, grew more serious. "You

should be prepared to meet her, Coren. Your future wife. I know you've been thinking about her."

Coren felt himself turn red. His thoughts about that girl were private—or ought to be. This was exactly what he hated most—people always nosing around your thoughts, ferreting out your deepest, most embarrassing secrets. It wasn't fair!

"Nonsense," Queen Milda said complacently, "it's perfectly fair. It's perfectly natural. It's the way things are, and that's that. And anyway, there's nothing for you to be embarrassed about. It's absolutely normal to feel that way about a girl before you meet her. And to think those kinds of thoughts. Everyone does it, I've been in all the young men's minds and I know."

She knew? She knew those thoughts, too? He felt himself turn even more red.

"And if you think you've got thoughts to be embarrassed about, Coren, well, let me tell you! Some of those boys' minds could stand a trip through the laundry—with lots of bleach and two rinses. I can promise you that you've no reason to be nervous. Lenora's bound to like you. You're a fine young man, the cream of Andillan manhood. Oh, I suppose you could learn to unbend a little now and then, but why would she not like you?"

Look in the mirror, Coren thought to himself miserably. Luckily, his mother was too caught up in her own thoughts to hear him.

"And you'll like her, too," she was saying. "She's a real princess, Lenora is, despite her, um, her little disability. A real princess." Coren could feel his mother's pride in the good match radiate through his mind, like heat from a fire. "Well," she finally said, "I hope you feel better now that we've had this little chat. You do, don't you?"

There was a brief silence as Coren willed himself to think pleasant thoughts, positive thoughts—anything to reassure Queen Milda and get her out of there.

"Well," he heard her say finally, "I guess that will have to do. And I am not a nosy old snoop, mister, and don't you forget it. And besides, I like those freckles. They remind me of your father."

And then she was, thankfully, gone from his head.

Coren sighed. Typical of his mother to invade his privacy just to make him feel better, which always made him feel worse.

And yet, he wondered uneasily, after he settled down in Gepeth, wouldn't he miss her popping up like that unexpectedly, just a little bit? When she was no longer in his mind anymore, would he want her back again? And all the rest of them, too? What would it be like never to have them there?

Well, what did it matter? The girl would no doubt hate him and call the marriage off the second she saw him. He sighed, then took a step forward to retrieve the razor he'd thrown down into the foliage, stumbled over a tree root, and fell.

"Ouch," the tree root thought.

Coren wished this horrible day was over.

4

"It was a sending—it had to be." After listening with rapt attention to Lenora's report of her strange experience, Lufa seemed even more solemn than she'd been earlier. She dipped the edge of her skirt into the pool and then bathed Lenora's temples with cold water as she considered what it could mean.

"Yes," she explained, "a sending. A vision someone sent to you, to show you—." She paused, and then her face grew more alarmed. "It must be a moment from the future—your future, Lenora, or at least a possible future, one you might choose. It's been sent to warn you, perhaps, or to prepare you—so that you'll be ready for it when it comes."

Ready for it? Ready for what? What had pulled her like that? Lenora shuddered.

"But who sent it?" Lufa mused. "And why did it come to you? The yearning in you, the discontent—whoever is doing it knows you might respond."

Would she? By now Lenora's teeth were chattering. She felt cold all over. Never had she thought she could feel such joy in evil, in destruction. Was she losing control of her mind?

And yet—the joy, the sheer joy of it. The power. Her teeth chattered even more.

Lufa caught Lenora's hand in hers.

"You can go there, Lenora," Lufa stated with certainty. "When the moment comes, you'll be able to go, if you wish to. It's a real place, I'm sure of that. And it's clear you're wanted there."

"But why? What for?" Lenora cried.

Lufa looked unsure. "For your power, perhaps."

"But that's silly. There's nothing special about my power!"

Then she remembered her mother's words: "You have more power than is good for anyone!"

Perhaps her mother was right. Perhaps she was on a dangerous road. How could she enjoy all that destruction so much? She had reveled in it. And something inside her, even now, wanted to experience it again. It was so confusing.

"Never mind, child," Lufa said in a soothing voice. "It's only a sending. It can't harm you, it can't draw you in, not unless you want it to. All you need to do is ignore it, and then everything will be fine."

But Lenora couldn't help noticing the troubled look in Lufa's eyes.

"Come on, up you get," Lufa commanded, pulling Lenora by the hand. "A brisk walk, blood flowing again, you'll be right as rain." She handed Lenora her basket and set off at a slow trot. Lenora followed. She had to force herself to keep up, but soon she was warmer, and she could feel the color returning to her cheeks.

They emerged from the garden just in time to catch the glint of horses' bridles on the road below. The king's party was returning. Lenora was surprised—she hadn't expected her father back from his hunting expedition for at least a few more days.

As soon as Lufa saw the king's party, her attitude changed. "Go to the kitchen and get some hot soup," she ordered, "and you'll be fine. And," she added hesitantly, "my best wishes, Lenora." Then she took the basket from Lenora and hurried toward her cottage.

Actually, Lenora already felt fine. The combination of exercise and her youth had quickly dispelled the sending and its aftereffects. As she sauntered back home, the sun beating down on her and warming her even more, she vaguely wondered why Lufa had rushed away so quickly, and why she'd wished her well.

She could see her father's party galloping up to the house on the road below her. If she hurried, she could reach the stables behind the palace at the same time as he did. At least, she thought as she began to run, the afternoon is almost over, and I've managed to keep out of trouble.

She reached the stable just as her father's party did,

and she ran across the stable yard to greet him as he dismounted from his horse and turned toward her.

King Rayden was a thin wiry man, with fair hair and blue eyes that were never at rest. His energy was boundless. "Lenora, my dear," he said, his voice jovial, "I've brought someone for you to meet. You'll never guess who. I wanted to surprise you. Your seventeenth birthday is fast approaching, and . . ." he paused. "You see, I haven't really been on a hunting trip. Well"—he laughed, looking at his men—"maybe I have." He chortled with obvious delight. "And I've bagged something just for you!"

At that he strode over to a figure standing next to one of the horses, fiddling with the saddle, apparently trying to melt out of sight.

"A husband!" King Rayden proclaimed.

A husband? Did he say a husband? Lenora stood in shocked silence as her father grabbed the figure by the shoulder and spun him around.

"And this is he!" he announced. "Lenora, dear, meet Prince Coren, son of Arno and Milda of Andilla."

Red hair, gray-blue eyes, white skin, freckles.

As she stared at the prince, the blood drained from her face. It was him. It was the boy she'd seen in the sending!

She turned with a choking sound and fled up the back stairs and into the palace.

❖ ❖ ❖

Coren clutched the stirrup of his horse, the only thing close enough to hold on to as his knees buckled under him. It was her. The young woman from that strange fantasy in the forest. It was her, the Princess Lenora. His fiancée.

The horse whinnied and moved, throwing Coren off balance. He let go of the stirrup and swayed unsteadily. King Rayden caught him under his arm.

"You all right, boy?"

Coren nodded dumbly. But he wasn't. He wasn't the least bit all right. It was bad enough that he'd just had that strange fantasy about her, but her reaction to his arrival was worse, far worse. A fitting end to a horrible journey.

Suddenly his mother was in his head again.

"Pull yourself together, Coren. Your lack of self-confidence is astonishing. You spend altogether too much time in your own thoughts."

Then he heard her turning her attention toward his father, voicing her outrage at the girl's rude behavior.

"You're right, Milda," King Arno declared inside his wife's and son's heads. "We're not beggars. Rayden came to us with this proposal, not the other way around. We don't need them."

"Well," Queen Milda huffed, "I've never seen anything like it. Just who does she think she is?"

King Rayden let go of Coren, rushed over to Queen

Milda in a tizzy, and tried to apologize for Lenora.

"Honestly," he protested, "I can't imagine what got into her. Perhaps it was the surprise."

"You didn't tell her?" Queen Milda was so shocked that she actually spoke aloud. Her voice rang out so that all could hear. Coren realized that he'd hardly ever heard it before—she never actually talked when she could just slip her way into someone's mind. She must be furious.

"Well," King Rayden answered, shifting nervously from one foot to the next, "we thought she should meet Coren, get to know him, see what a nice harmless boy he is, and then we'd tell her. But when I saw her just now, I couldn't resist saying something. I was so pleased. Mistake, I suppose. She can be a bit headstrong."

Coren was so angry King Rayden had called him harmless that he almost missed the headstrong part. But his parents were eyeing King Rayden thoughtfully.

"Headstrong? He neglected to mention that before," Coren overheard Queen Milda say inside King Arno's mind.

"Indeed," said his father aloud. He had obviously decided the situation had gone beyond politeness, and was now shamelessly investigating King Rayden's thoughts. "Yes, yes," he said to King Rayden. "I see there's a lot you never mentioned. Talking chairs, indeed. Dragons in the laundry room, humph. I see I was making a mistake, being polite enough not to read what was really on your mind."

"Yes," said Queen Milda, speaking aloud again, "or else we'd have known about the Luxorian ambassador turning into a goat."

"And about the pond in the garden turning into lemonade," King Arno added.

The Luxorian ambassador? Lemonade? Coren was flabbergasted. He was engaged to a girl who turned ponds into lemonade?

So it was true. It had to be true. She did have something to do with those nightmarish visions. It had been her in that pool, after all. Was it possible?

Well, that was it. The very last straw. There was no way he was going to marry her. White bears. Pink puppies. Lemonade. Pools, dangerous pools. He would tell his parents. As soon as they were alone. Or maybe tonight.

Or tomorrow, perhaps, after they got over being so angry about how King Rayden had tricked them.

"Wait," King Rayden said hastily. "Let me go after her. I'll speak to her, and I promise that by tonight everything will be fine."

Before anybody could object, King Rayden called for servants to escort his guests to their quarters and bounded up the stairway into the house, leaving behind a very angry king and queen, and a very upset young prince.

5

This banquet is a disaster, Lenora told herself, a complete and total disaster. Just like the rest of my day. I have to get out of here.

She was sitting beside Prince Coren on the high dais in front of everybody, just as her parents had insisted, and she was being polite. Nothing more, just polite—but, she told herself, he was lucky to get even politeness, showing up like that out of nowhere and demanding she marry him. As if she were a piece of dry goods or something!

That's just what she'd said to her father. Told him he was treating her like dry goods. She trembled with anger as she remembered that horrible encounter. He'd been so furious with her for running from Prince Coren that he'd stormed into her room without even knocking, grabbed her arm, and told her that he'd never seen such disgraceful behavior in his life.

Well, how was she supposed to react? A husband, of all things. And they hadn't even asked her about it. They gave her no more consideration than they'd give a bolt of gabardine. No, she wasn't sorry she'd returned her father's anger with her own, even though her hand still smarted from the blow she'd given her bedroom wall. With a mixture of pride and dismay, she remembered the crater she'd created in the plaster, not with her mind but with her fist. You could see the wood lath right through it.

After that, her father had suddenly become very calm, too calm. He'd told her she was completely out of control and that only marriage could save her from herself.

"No question about it, young lady," he'd said, "it's time you grew up. And marriage will do it. Once you're married, you'll be too busy running a household to worry about adventure."

Furthermore, it had to be marriage to someone like Coren.

"Oh," King Rayden had said, "his people are a little flighty, I don't deny it. But luckily, Coren seems to have escaped the family character, even if he does share their handicap."

Handicap? What did that mean, she wondered, taking a furtive glance at the frail figure seated beside her. Could all those freckles be considered a handicap? Well, they seemed to run in the family. His father had them, too.

Anyway, King Rayden had announced that the wedding—her wedding—would take place in just two weeks. And then he'd left her there, stewing in her room, staring at the hole in the wall, too angry to even think, while he went to smooth things over with Prince Coren's parents.

Apparently he'd succeeded—at least enough for them to agree to come to this miserable banquet and force her to sit there in front of everybody like some mindless little doll, ever so politely asking this Coren person to "please pass the sauceboat, if you'd be so kind," and pretending not to notice how he spent the whole time hunched over his plate, deliberately ignoring her. It was the perfect end to a perfect day.

A sharp ringing noise interrupted Lenora's thoughts. It was her father, now on his feet, tapping his wineglass with his spoon to get everybody's attention. Oh no, please, not that! Surely he wasn't going to make a speech.

He was. In a panic, Lenora spun around to see how Prince Coren was going to respond to her father's embarrassing behavior. As she turned, he turned toward her. They were looking directly at one another.

And she wasn't seeing a pathetic, skinny boy who was too shy to even talk about the weather. She was seeing a strong, compassionate face, she was looking into sympathetic gray-blue eyes. She felt something, something—

No. She didn't. She didn't feel anything. She blinked, shook her head, and quickly turned away.

"Princess?" It was the prince's voice, low and concerned. "Are you all right?"

She had to get out of there. Murmuring the briefest of apologies, she arose from the table and dashed from the dining room as fast as her shaky legs would carry her.

Once in her room, she slammed the door behind her and leaned against it, panting. Everyone was probably furious with her, all over again. Well, she wasn't going to dwell on it. And she certainly wasn't going to think about him. He wasn't worth the effort. There wasn't even one hair growing on his immature face.

No, she had to focus on what to do now. How to get away from Coren and from everything he represented. She perched on the edge of the small couch by the fire and stared into the flames.

There was obviously only one thing to do, she decided. She would change her reality. It was her only option, if she really wanted to escape. She would imagine that the world was different, better. Without all these silly confusions.

But, she realized with a sinking feeling, it wouldn't work. The least smidgen of an attempt to change reality, and her father would simply stop her. Unfortunately, he was still more powerful than she was.

Unless she could change the world so completely that he, too, would be changed! She might make him into a weakling like that Coren, or even better, some harmless kind of animal or something. King Rayden the pet squirrel. And everyone except her would believe that things had always been that way.

She had a brief vision of a world where everything was orderly, where she was in charge, where people cringed as she walked by, where her power was immense.

No, no, that reminded her too much of the sending.

That sending. He was in it—Prince Coren. What had he been doing there? Could it possibly have come from him?

She dismissed the possibility, remembering the intense power of the vision. Not Coren. Somebody else. But still—why was Coren in it?

Well, Lufa had said it was from her future, or from a possible future—and maybe that future was beginning to happen. Because now she knew who the boy in the sending was. She had actually met him.

Coren. Those eyes—they were very intense. She gave her head a small shake and went back to considering possible ways of changing the world.

She would be rich. Everyone else would be poor, including her father, and she'd give them food, and they'd thank her and worship her and bow down when she passed and—

No, that was silly. She didn't have the strength to change everything in this world.

But instead, maybe she could picture a different world and then throw herself into it. That way she wouldn't have to change everybody else. She could just leave them behind here, happy in their boring old balanced existence, while she herself went on to better things.

And so she did. She was queen. She sat on a throne in a beautiful palace. Ladies and gentleman of the court milled around her. A young man walked up to her, his doublet carelessly open to reveal a muscular chest. He had thick wavy black hair, deep blue eyes, a square jaw, broad shoulders, and a very slim waist.

"Your Majesty," he crooned as he bent over her hand to kiss it.

"Sir knight," she sighed, gazing at him with pleasure.

But then, could it be? His hair slowly began to change color—black slowly became brown, then red. The pure skin became spotted with freckles. The eyes became more gray than blue, and for a moment she looked into them and again was caught, despite herself, by something, something deeper than infatuation—

This wasn't what she'd planned! It was all wrong. Her mind must be wandering to create such nonsense. She blotted it all out and found herself once more in front of the fire, the heat warming her skin.

Well, she didn't need a handsome knight, did she?

She didn't need anybody else in order to be happy. She'd live alone on an island, and she'd hunt and fish and ride. She'd take care of herself, and she'd need no one.

Within seconds she was there—standing outside a beautiful cottage, a lake glistening in the sunset, the sky turning shades of pink and purple on the horizon and a deep royal blue overhead, a basket of berries in her hand. She turned to walk into the cottage. The smell of fresh piecrust was everywhere. She opened the door, and Coren grinned at her from the kitchen as he wiped a powdery hand across his forehead, leaving ridiculous patches of white on his face and hair.

"No!" she exclaimed in astonishment. "Not you! What are you doing here?"

"Waiting for my blackberries," he answered, "and if you don't hurry you'll ruin all my hard work."

"No, no, no!" she screamed and found herself back in front of the fire.

What's going on? she thought desperately. Why is he turning up like this in my creations? It's from my mind, and I don't want him there! Of all people in the world he's the one I least want there!

She paused. I have to calm down, she thought. I have to think of somewhere—she had an idea. Fine, if he insists on being in my creation he'll have his wish—but I'll control it! I'll control him!

She imagined a huge castle. She was riding a beautiful black mare up to the castle gates. Situated just on her right was a small hut with bars on the windows and a guard at the door. She glanced over. Coren looked at her through the bars. She laughed in delight.

"There!" she cried aloud to him in triumph. "If I can't get rid of you, I can at least put you where you belong. How does it feel to be a prisoner?"

But to her dismay, he answered her. She hadn't planned for him to answer her.

"I hate it," he groaned. "Please let me go." And he looked at her with those compelling eyes, and she felt sorry for him.

She didn't want to feel sorry for him. She wanted him out of her thoughts.

Abruptly the prison was gone, and the horse and the castle, too. But those eyes were still there, those deep blue eyes. She was imprisoned by those eyes. He was her jailer.

Why couldn't she stop thinking about that idiot? She had to escape from him.

Escape. As she thought the word, wishing for release, she suddenly saw the pool and heard voices chanting. She was back in the sending, being pulled, being drawn to a beautiful vision of great joy and great power, paradise—

Then, just as quickly, it was gone. She was back by the fire. Alone.

She sighed and sank onto the couch. She didn't like that vision. Or rather, she was confused by it. It disturbed her that it had, once more, come into her head unbidden. And it was enticing, it tantalized her. She wanted it, and she didn't want it.

But she had no time to think about that vision now. She had to get away. And she had an idea—real escape, using her own two legs. She would run away. And she would do it now, tonight, before anyone expected it, before they could stop her. She'd run away to a different land where people lived in different ways. She'd get as far away from Coren and marriage as possible.

Quickly she moved around the room, preparing her escape. It had to be right. It had to be all real—nothing imagined, nothing created. She rummaged through the closet, choosing a leather riding skirt and a warm black sweater and a black leather jerkin. She also put on her riding boots and a peaked cap. In a small bag she packed clean underclothes, two dresses, a pair of shoes, and an extra sweater—and, as an afterthought, all her gold jewelry.

She knew she should feel some regret at leaving her parents and for the worry she would cause them, but she felt none. She only wanted to be away from the stifling life they had planned for her.

And away from Prince Coren. Why had he entered her worlds like that, spoiling her creations? Well, she thought, at least he'd never know about it, at least she'd be spared that embarrassment.

The palace seemed quiet. She put on her cap and moved to her door, tiptoeing on the balls of her feet so that her boot heels wouldn't click on the tiled floor.

6

Coren stared glumly into the fire, hardly conscious of the wonderfully soft bed he was sitting on. It was hard to enjoy all these luxuries when life was so confusing.

At supper, for a moment, when their eyes had met, he thought Princess Lenora might actually be feeling something for him. He'd seen—something in her eyes.

But then she'd shut him out and bolted from the room, just as if she were frightened of him. Frightened of him, of all things.

It was only fair. He was frightened of her, too. She was a frightening person. That vision he had somehow picked up before they actually met—it must have been some nightmarish fantasy she had invented of herself staring into a pool. Well, it only made sense to be frightened of somebody who could imagine something as strange as that.

Yet, when he'd looked into her eyes, he'd felt such a rush of emotion he could barely contain it. Was this love? Surely not. He couldn't love her.

And she couldn't possibly love him.

Not that he'd know if she did. He prided himself on that. He'd been extra careful at dinner not to enter her thoughts uninvited. That was impolite, no matter what his mother and father said. And who knows what embarrassing thoughts about himself he might over-hear.

He had managed fairly well, too—until she had let him in of her own accord. But it was a brief encounter, too short for him to do more than sense something, something—

Something unexpected. Something he didn't understand.

Whatever it was, her sudden flight from the ban-quet had caused such a commotion that he hadn't had any time to think about it. What with his mother chat-tering wildly away inside his father's mind and his own about how erratic Lenora was, and Queen Savet blush-ing in embarrassment and doing her best to pretend nothing unusual had happened, and King Rayden try-ing to reassure everybody by telling bad jokes and laughing too loud—well, in all that tumult it was impossible to think about anything.

The commotion had brought the banquet to an immediate halt. Now that he was back in his room, he couldn't stop thinking about her.

Her eyes. He could see them clearly in his mind, just as if she were actually there. Those eyes were shin-ing under the elaborate jeweled crown she wore on her head. She was a queen. She sat at a throne in a beautiful palace. Ladies and gentlemen of the court milled around her. Without even willing it, Coren found himself walking up to her, bending over her hand to kiss it, then looking up to see the furious look on her face just as it disappeared from view and he found himself staring into the fire again.

Wait a minute. What was happening?

Before Coren could even begin to think about it, he realized that he was looking at Lenora again. She was right there, in front of him, and he was grinning at her, and he was in the middle of baking a pie.

But I don't know how to bake a pie, he told himself hysterically. How much flour should I use?

But there was no time to worry about flour. He wasn't baking a pie, after all. He was staring into a fire, suddenly back in his bedroom.

Coren took a deep breath and willed himself not to panic. Then he tried to understand what was happening to him. He sent his mind out searching and quickly found the explanation. Lenora was in her own room, and she was thinking about him—and every time she did, he was a captive in her head, thinking her thoughts, living her fantasies. He was being dragged into her mind completely against his will. Why? Why was it happening?

He lay there on the bed, desperately trying to resist the pull of her mind. But he couldn't. He was being caught, trapped again and again, unable to do anything but watch helplessly as he became the leading character in all her schemes to escape. And she didn't seem to like it any more than he did—now she had him in some kind of smelly prison, and the look on her face on the other side of the bars was dangerous indeed.

He grabbed on to the cold iron bars and tried to reason with her, to calm her down. It didn't work, though. She was furious with him. She was shouting at him angrily—something about being a jailer, something about escape.

And then, suddenly, his hands were gripping nothing. The bars had disappeared, and the prison and Lenora with them. He was back on the bed again. Released from prison. Released from the prison of Lenora's thoughts.

He lay there for some time, his heart pounding, waiting. Any minute now it would happen again, he thought, but it didn't. This time, it seemed, she was gone, really gone. Coren stood up, still shaking, still certain that at any moment he might be pulled away again.

He couldn't stand it. He had to know. He sent his thoughts out again, searching for Lenora. There she was, still in her room. And thinking, apparently, about clothes now, not about him. Good. For a while, at least, he was safe.

This is ridiculous, he told himself. She thinks of me

as her jailer, and meanwhile she's imprisoning me in her thoughts. I don't want to be her jailer. I definitely don't want to be jailed by her. I don't want anything but to get out of this place and go home and forget about her altogether.

I'll tell her, he said to himself. Not inside her head, she'll think I'm just a fantasy again. No, I'll go to her in person. I'll let her know that she can escape anytime she wants to, that it's just fine by me, that I don't want to marry her any more than she wants to marry me. And then maybe she'll stop pulling me into her head this way.

And before he could talk himself out of it, he got up from his bed, left his room, and stepped out into the darkened corridor.

The passageway was empty. Slowly Lenora moved through the corridor to the stairs, which were lit by small candles placed in holders on the walls.

She was almost free.

And then there was a terrible crash, and a scream.

Lenora froze. Doors opened all along the hall, and within seconds, worried servants with candles hovered around her, seeking the source of the loud noise. Moments later her father strode into view, took in her traveling clothes with one quick glance, and demanded, "Lenora, what is the meaning of this?"

"Sire," a breathless young servant interrupted. "The

noise—it was Prince Coren. He tripped on the landing and crashed into the queen's blue vase. He sends his sincere apologies."

Coren. Again.

Lenora's shoulders sagged. She had been caught—and it was all that miserable boy's fault. What a clumsy oaf he was. And what was he doing skulking through the corridors in the middle of the night like some criminal?

"Lenora," her father said quietly, "please return to your room. And prepare. The ceremony will take place tomorrow morning."

Then he turned to the servants. "I want no talk of this little indiscretion to our visitors," he ordered. "They are not to know."

The servants nodded and dispersed, all except two of King Rayden's most trusted men. They escorted Lenora back to her room and placed themselves on either side of the door in the corridor. She was a prisoner now. Despairing, Lenora went into her room and threw herself on her bed.

Changing this world was impossible. Creating another one was worse. And escape was out. She was trapped.

7

I'm an idiot, Coren berated himself, a complete idiot. Useless even at walking around in the dark. No wonder she wants to get away from me.

And she did, more than ever. Now that he was back in his room, he was being drawn into her thoughts again, pulled against his will like iron filings by a magnet. He had no choice but to eavesdrop as she told herself how furious she was with the hateful villain who stopped her escape. Him, she meant.

He shut his eyes. What should he do? Just refuse to marry her? She obviously wasn't what he wanted in a wife—just the opposite, in fact. Life with someone as headstrong and imaginative as Lenora certainly wasn't going to be the safe, solid existence he'd hoped for— not when she could change it all at any moment, transform it into every sort of nightmarish horror.

Once more the memory of that vision in the mirror passed through his mind, and he shivered.

And yet, this was astonishing, he found part of himself somehow not wanting to give it all up—not Gepeth, not even Lenora. Part of him found it all exhilarating—in a nerve-racking sort of way.

And, yes, he also had to admit that he wanted to see Lenora again. He was drawn to her. It was terrifying, the way she pulled him to her, but it was wonderful at the same time. The intensity of her thoughts, the rich texture of them. It was definitely better than any fantasy book he'd ever read.

On the other hand, she wanted nothing to do with him. She hated him. Of course she did, he'd given her no reason not to. He sighed. Best just to refuse the marriage, for her sake if not for his own.

His eyes were finally growing heavy. He was free of her mind now, back in his own dull, safe thoughts—perhaps she'd finally managed to fall asleep. He sank back onto the thick down comforter. It felt marvelous, especially since for once in his life he wasn't tempted to think a rough, threadbare blanket into something softer and warmer.

A pity to give solid luxuries like this up, really. But the marriage was impossible. She wasn't for him, and that was that. He'd do it. Tomorrow. He sighed and fell asleep.

"Time to get up, Miss Lenora," Marlia said, drawing back the covers. "Your bath is ready and your mother is on her way to talk to you."

I wonder, thought Lenora as she yawned and stretched, what Prince Coren really thinks about all this. I suppose he always does just what

Mommy and Daddy tell him to do.

Well, she thought defiantly, they'll be sorry in the end, because this stupid marriage won't last long. I can't run away from here, maybe—but I can run away from Coren after we're married. He can't keep me a prisoner in my own home, he wouldn't have the strength. That thought cheered her a little.

Just then Lenora's mother swept into the room. She had a small frown on her face. She looked at Lenora, then away.

"What is it, Mother?" Lenora said, knowing Queen Savet well enough to sense that something was very wrong.

Queen Savet sat on the small couch, gesturing for Lenora to sit beside her.

"Give her a shawl, Marlia," the queen ordered as Lenora obeyed and sat beside her. "Do you want her to catch a chill?" Her voice was shrill.

It was warm in the room, and Lenora was perfectly comfortable in her cotton nightshirt, but she allowed Marlia to place a heavy wool shawl over her shoulders. Her mother took her hand.

"Lenora, you worried your father terribly when you tried to run away. It's a dangerous world outside of Gepeth. You have no idea—your life has been so safe, so secure." She paused.

Lenora didn't speak. She wanted to say, yes, too safe, too secure, but she refrained. She sensed her mother was working up to saying something important and probably unpleasant.

"Lenora, there's something I have to tell you." She sighed, then spoke quickly. "As part of your dowry, your father has given Prince Coren the island of Crosnor, and his parents have agreed that you both will live there until after your second child is born. At that point, you'll return to the mainland and take up Prince Coren's lands and holdings. The boats, which are the only transportation to and from the island, will be under constant guard by your father's own men. And—"

Her mother hesitated, apparently unwilling to tell her something even worse. "And there will be a brigade posted on the mainland, using its mental power to hold you there."

A whole brigade? Outrageous. Well, that was the last straw. Abruptly, Lenora withdrew her hand from her mother's.

"I have to take my bath," she stated flatly. And without so much as another glance at her mother she got up and marched from the room.

"Wake up," King Arno shouted as he pulled the prince out of a deep sleep, his voice rumbling through Coren's mind. "You'll never guess what."

His father's news was no surprise to Coren—he had all too clear memories of the colorful, enraged thoughts he'd been forced to overhear in Lenora's mind after that ugly blue vase had suddenly appeared out of nowhere and King Rayden had discovered his daughter in the corridor and made his decision about moving up the ceremony. But Coren wasn't going to go through with it no matter how much his parents insisted on it, and that was that. Because, he told himself, they would insist on it. It was a good political move, good for both countries. Furthermore, King Rayden had misread Coren's parents if he'd thought they'd be put off by Lenora's childhood escapades. Once they got over the shock of being lied to like that, they were bound to see her as an even better match—she was even crazier than they were themselves, if that was possible. Oh yes, now that they knew about the talking chairs and all, they were going to be even more anxious for the marriage to take place.

But his father surprised him.

"The young lady isn't at all what we were led to believe," King Arno said. "She's headstrong and imaginative. I'd expected her to be boring, like everyone else here. And she certainly isn't boring."

No, Coren thought ruefully, she certainly isn't boring.

"No, she isn't," his father agreed. "And that's just it, isn't it? Your mother and I felt, well, we felt that someone boring would suit you just fine. That's what we thought, isn't it, Milda?"

"Yes." He could see his mother's face beside his father's in his mind, nodding in agreement.

"So," his father continued, "the question is, will the Princess Lenora suit you? Well, Coren, we've decided we won't force you."

"It's up to you," his mother added. "We're leaving it up to you."

He was free. His parents weren't going to force him to marry this upsetting girl after all, and he didn't even have to defy them about it.

So he opened his mouth to reply and said, "I'll marry her."

It was more of a shock to himself than it was to his parents. He must have lost his mind.

His parents, though, were delighted. So delighted, in fact, that they hurried away before he could reverse his decision, leaving him with no choice but to go through with it.

And, he added to himself as he put on the strange and very uncomfortable suit that King Rayden had sent for him to wear at the ceremony, I hope Lenora doesn't hate me for it too much. I hope I don't hate me for it too much.

But he couldn't picture leaving her, despite the merry dance he'd been led ever since he'd first heard of her, despite the strange time he'd spent unwillingly in her mind.

Even despite the tormented dreams he'd just been

experiencing. Nightmares about that pool, about water rippling, about terrible danger.

Was Lenora in danger? Was he? He hoped not. He wasn't ready for danger. And yet he felt that they were somehow tied together, he and Lenora. It wasn't love, of course, nothing like that. But there was something there, something pulling him to her. And he couldn't, apparently, resist—not even if he wanted to.

And so, somewhat bewildered, Coren soon found himself standing by the altar, clothed in an uncomfortable garment of powder blue that revealed all too clearly how ridiculously skinny his legs were, awaiting his marriage.

Lenora was feeling numb rather than angry. It was all over, then. Any chance of escape gone. And if she and Coren had children, she wouldn't be able to leave them. That's what her father was counting on, and he was probably right.

She allowed herself to be bathed, dressed, even fed. It was all as in a dream, a dream happening to someone else. Finally, she was led downstairs by Marlia and her mother's other servants, to wait for the carriage that would take her to the chapel in the village.

"You look lovely, miss," Marlia whispered to her as she descended the stairs.

Lenora looked at herself in the full-length mirror on the landing. She did look nice, she thought, as though commenting on a stranger. Her hair was threaded with gold braid. A gold necklace at her throat just touched the white lace of her gown. The gown her mother had given her to wear was the one she herself had been married in. It was low at the neck, tucked in under the breasts, flowing at the ground, delicate lace, patterned over silk. Interwoven in the lace was gleaming gold thread, which brought out the gleam of her hair. It was almost as beautiful as the dresses she'd imagined for herself. Not that she cared.

Her father was waiting for her outside the door of the chapel in the village. He smiled with delight when he saw how lovely she looked. She put her hand on his arm, mechanically, and didn't acknowledge him. He patted her hand.

"I know you," he soothed. "You feel you hate me now, but this is for the best. You'll see. And I promise to be the most doting of grandfathers."

She didn't respond, she couldn't. She couldn't allow herself to get angry, it made everything too difficult. She knew she had to remain numb and unfeeling or she wouldn't survive the day.

The choir began to sing, the organ to play. The heavy wooden doors opened. Slowly, she and her father moved down the aisle of the chapel. She'd seen it so many times before, but never had she understood it like this.

The long central aisle—perfect for a father to

march his daughter down against her will.

The pews on both sides of the aisle filled with all the people of the court, hastily gathered to witness her humiliation and make sure she couldn't escape.

Down at the end of the aisle, Agneth, the Keeper of the Balance, who put her to sleep with his boring and endless sermons week after weary week and who was about to imprison her in the balance forever.

And there, behind Agneth, the stone basin filled with water, resting on a thick stone base. How many times had she watched her many cousins marry and heard Agneth repeat that the water signified the purity of their vows, and how, like water, they must in marriage be willing to join different paths into one path, adapt, be fluid—keep the balance.

As Lenora walked past the front row, she noted in passing that her future in-laws were dressed in peculiar, tattered clothes. Her mother gave her a warm encouraging smile. Lenora stared right through her.

Prince Coren was waiting at the altar, standing in front of Agneth. He, at least, was wearing a half-decent suit, a powder blue one in the most current of Gepethian styles. He really looked quite good in it, too, despite his skinny legs. Not that she cared, of course.

Her father took her hand from his arm and placed it firmly on Prince Coren's. The prince glanced at her and then quickly turned to Agneth, who had already begun the ceremony.

The Keeper droned on and on, for what seemed to Lenora to be an eternity. Finally, he came to the water sanctification.

"Move forward, my children," said Agneth, "and observe your future."

Without even thinking about it, Lenora moved up to the basin and peered in. She saw her own reflection—and there, behind it, Coren's face, rippling in the water.

Suddenly she snapped out of her lassitude. It was her vision. This was the moment of the sending!

The water swirled. She heard a voice. She was being called, beckoned. Quickly she scanned the room. No one else could see or hear anything, she was sure of it. But she could feel the water, the vision pulling her.

And she wanted to go. After all, what could be worse than this? What?

A little piece of her mind protested and said, Wait, not this, if you wish to flee, create something of your own, this isn't yours, you don't know what it is. But, she thought, I can't create my own, I've tried, someone is offering me something and it's my chance to escape. I just have to say yes.

She could feel Coren's hand on her arm.

"No," she heard him say. "No, don't do it!"

"I will," she cried. "I have to!" And with that she threw her mind into the sending, and her body followed.

She could hear Coren calling. Then she was no longer in the chapel, no longer with her parents. She was perched on a rock looking over an endless sea.

And Coren was sitting next to her.

8

"**A**re you mad?" she screamed at him. "Why did you follow me? I jumped into this just to get away from you!"

Lenora turned away from Coren in fury and looked out over the unfamiliar landscape below them. The hill they were perched on was the only elevated land for as far as she could see in any direction. On one side of the hill, far below, was the sea, stretching off into the gray distance, but the other side was totally different. At the end of an absolutely straight road that ran like a ribbon across a flat, open plain, a city arose, gleaming and shimmering, tall white spires shooting up into the low clouds, a city like nothing she'd seen before.

"It's beautiful—so beautiful," she said, her eyes soaking in the grandeur of the towers.

Then her glance fell on Coren again, and her delight withered.

"Not that it matters how beautiful it is," she announced. "You've spoiled it. I leap into another world, and you just chase after me like some mindless puppy. Well, it's no good with you here, no good at all.

I'm going home right now, and you're coming with me whether you like it or not. And I'm putting my foot down. I don't care what they say, I will not marry! Not you or anybody! They can't make me, they can't, they can't, they can't! And then—" her eyes wandered back to the white towers—"maybe I'll come back here again. On my own."

She grabbed Coren's hand before he could object, closed her eyes, willed the picture of her home into her mind, and leaped.

A gray wall seemed to crash down around her, preventing any movement. She was still there, still standing on that hill and still holding Coren's hand.

"What's happened?" he asked in a shaky voice. "There we were in the . . . and then . . . I don't understand." His words turned into a weak whimper.

What a bumbling idiot he was! She had to get the poor scared creature out of here. She closed her eyes and tried once more. Again, she experienced her body and spirit being slammed into a fixed grayness which held her. Her powers weren't working.

They had always worked before.

"This is ridiculous," she protested. "I want to go home, and I'm going."

Again she tried, this time slowly and carefully creating a detailed image in her mind of her parents, the chapel, the pool she had moved through. It was there, it was almost—

Wham!

She dropped Coren's hand, staggered back, and sank to the ground.

"I—I can't do it. I can't leave."

Coren stared down at her, torn between his own fear and his concern for her. Lenora actually seemed frightened. She needed his help.

"Are—are you all right?" He tentatively reached out to touch her.

But before he could, she looked up at him with fury in her eyes. "All right? All right? Of course I'm not all right." She pulled herself to her feet and paced back and forth over the rocky ground as she hissed angry words at him. "My powers aren't working. We're stuck here! I'm stuck here—with you!"

Well, Coren thought ruefully, at least she was back to herself again. He could stop worrying about her being frightened and go back to being frightened himself.

"Stuck where?" he asked, looking anxiously out over the strange landscape. "Where are we?"

She turned and glared into his face. "Where are we indeed! You might well ask!" Then her eyes lost their fire.

"I don't know where we are," she muttered. She turned and slowly walked away from him, her shoulders slumped.

"You don't know?"

"That's right. I don't know. It wasn't my vision. I was so desperate I just leaped into what I saw in the pool."

Coren was astonished. She just leaped, without looking first?

"That was pretty foolish," he blurted out.

"Foolish!" Lenora blazed. "And just what choice did I have? Stand there and get forced into marriage?"

She was right. What could he have been thinking, agreeing to go ahead with it? And now look what had happened!

"But I don't understand," he said. "Why can't we go back?"

"I don't know," Lenora replied, her voice anxious. "I try, but I keep hitting some kind of wall."

"Then we're prisoners here?" Coren said, horrified.

Lenora glared at him. "I don't know! Maybe." She paused, and her eyes narrowed. "Just what are you doing here anyway?"

"I—well, I sensed danger. I didn't want you to get hurt. I tried to stop you. I tried to pull you back." He sighed. "Instead, you pulled me along—or at least, I think you did." He looked at her in admiration. "You're far stronger than I am, obviously."

Lenora gave him a withering look. "You were trying to save me! You, the knight in shining armor, rescuing me, the poor little damsel in distress. How sweet!"

"I tried at least," Coren exclaimed. "There's no need to make fun of me. I just tried to help."

"Don't you see?" Lenora snapped. "I didn't want your help!"

"Yes," Coren grimaced. "I can see that now. It was stupid of me." And then, to himself, he added, really stupid. She didn't want his help. She didn't want anything to do with him. What had he been thinking of?

Still, he thought, there must be something I can do. If I can just keep calm and think it through. Because if we could figure out where we are, then we could maybe—

He had an idea. "Princess," he asked Lenora, "do you recognize this place? Is it one of your creations?"

"I've told you already," she exploded, exasperated. "No. Of course not."

"But think about it. How can you be sure? Maybe it's something from a dream, or something you aren't aware of, something from some hidden part of your mind?"

"That's ridiculous," she said.

Well, maybe so, Coren told himself, but if she wasn't aware of it, well, then of course she wouldn't know about it.

There was a way he could find out for sure, and now wasn't the time to be squeamish.

He sent his mind out to hers. He heard nothing. It was as if Lenora weren't even there.

And then, as if that weren't enough, he realized that the silence was everywhere. He could hear nothing at all—not even the rocks he and Lenora sat on or the feeble weeds at his feet. He had never before been so completely and utterly alone.

It was what he'd always wanted, what he'd hoped and wished for. He'd had no idea it would hurt so much. He sagged forward, holding his head in his hands in terrible agony.

"Prince Coren," Lenora said anxiously, "what is it?"

Well, he might as well tell her. His one strength, the one thing he had to offer, was gone.

"You see, I—well, I was trying to hear your thoughts, enter your mind."

Lenora gasped, astonished. "You were trying to do what?"

"You—you didn't know?" Why hadn't they told her? "We Andillans can hear one another's thoughts. It's an ability we're all born with, just like the way you people of Gepeth can imagine things into reality."

"You—you mean you can't imagine things and make them real?"

"No. Oh, of course, my people do imagine the places they live in, just as yours do. But the places we imagine have no real physical substance—they exist only in our thoughts."

This must be the handicap her father had spoken of, Lenora mused. How odd. To imagine things and yet still know that what you're imagining isn't really there. Still, the Andillans could hear others' thoughts. Now that would be an interesting gift to have, you could find out what other people were thinking about you, you could know all their private fears and worries and—

Suddenly, she turned and stared down into his earnest face, her eyes narrowing dangerously. Some of the thoughts she'd been having about Coren, about herself and him, had just passed through her mind.

"How dare you enter my private thoughts?" she said. "I won't stand for it! In fact, I refuse to be near you. I'll go somewhere where you can't hear me. Goodbye and good riddance!" And with that, she lifted the train of her gown up off the ground and began to stride purposefully down the hill.

No, no, thought Coren in a panic, she can't leave me, here, alone. Not even the air is talking! She can't! He quickly rose to his feet and shouted after her.

"Lenora," he called. "Wait, wait."

"Stay away!" she called over her shoulder. "Stay away from me! I'm not having some sneaky spy in my brain and that's that."

"Don't worry about it," he called out to her retreating back. "I can't hear anything now."

"What?" She quickly stopped and turned to stare at him.

"I only tried to enter your thoughts to see if this

place has something to do with a part of your mind that you aren't conscious of—but I couldn't hear a thing. Not even the air." He slumped down again. "My ability seems to have left me."

Lenora drew in a deep breath and started to move back toward him. She was about to scold him, but when she looked at his sagging shoulders she felt only pity.

She could help the poor fellow out, maybe. She could use her own gift to imagine his gift back for him. Except, of course, she'd make it so that he could read everyone's thoughts but hers. She shut her eyes and imagined him with his powers back.

"Well," she said, opening her eyes. "Can you hear anything now?"

"Not even the air," he said miserably.

And then she remembered that gray wall. She obviously had lost her own ability, just like him. She had to find out why—and the answer was bound to be below, in that city.

And, she supposed, looking into his forlorn face, she had better take the poor fellow with her. It seemed he was incapable of looking after himself.

"I'm sorry you're upset," she said. "I really am. But we can't just sit around and mope—that won't change anything." She pointed and began to move down the hill toward the city. "I'm heading off there, to find out what I can find out. Are you coming or not?" This last was flung over her shoulders.

For a brief moment, Coren couldn't decide. How could she just go tramping off like that into unknown territory? Someone or something had brought them here—someone or something unknown, someone or something with great power. And she was going to seek it out. Had she no prudence at all?

"I'm coming," he called miserably. "Wait for me!"

9

Lenora's spirits were beginning to lift dramatically. The view from the hill was lovely—the clouds were breaking up, leaving the sky a bright blue. The vast plain below rippled green in the breeze, and the towers gleamed off in the distance. And, she realized, there were no parents to tell her what to do, she didn't have to get married, anything might happen in this strange new place. It would be perfect if it weren't for the minor annoyance of Prince Coren following her around like a puppy. What was taking him so long anyway?

Yes, she was beginning to feel quite wonderful. She tramped down the hill, deliberately kicking her delicate white wedding slippers in the dirty gravel to get them as soiled as possible.

Suddenly she stopped dead in her tracks.

All around her, on the hill, people were appearing out of nowhere—much as she and Coren must have done. Hundreds of people.

Or were they people?

Lenora looked in astonishment at all the new arrivals. Yes, some were people, people of all ages, dressed in very different costumes, but if clothing meant anything, then they seemed to have one thing in common. None was poor. Their garments were made of silks, satins, and velvets; and although the designs differed, the quality did not. She could see they were, like her and Coren, from wealthy houses.

But as for the others—well, it was hard for her to tell what they were. Some looked vaguely human, except that the heads emerging from their opulent garments were huge and bald, and their skin was astonishing shades of rust and lemon and mauve. Others had delicate gauzy wings sprouting from their shoulders and were apparently wearing nothing at all. Others looked like lizards, with iridescent scales glinting in the light. Still others were short and stocky and had two or more heads. And here and there in the midst of them were clouds of vapor with lights twinkling in them, which may have been living creatures and may have been only clouds of swamp gas.

Before Lenora could even register her astonishment at this very odd crowd, it changed. In the blink of an eye, the gauzy vapors and shiny lizards and two-headed monsters disappeared, leaving only people—recognizable human beings wearing fine garments, looking for all the world as if they had gathered for a banquet or some other regal occasion. Lenora began to doubt that she had actually seen the other creatures. Might it have been just her imagination?

She quickly glanced back at Coren, wondering if he had seen them, too. He was still sitting on top of the hill—hadn't even managed to make it to his feet yet.

As she turned back, she could see the new arrivals standing for a moment, apparently too stunned to move. Then, almost as one, they began to walk toward the road that intersected the plain below. It seemed like a good idea. Bunching her dress up even further, and cursing its bulk, she fell in with the others hurrying toward the road.

Meanwhile, Coren sat on top of the hill, staring out at the strange conglomeration of people, his mind racing. Why had all those monsters blinked out, just as suddenly as the whole throng had appeared? Why had the throng appeared in the first place? And why couldn't he enter their minds and find out?

But there was no time to think about it. Lenora was already well ahead of him, totally unconcerned as to whether he was following or not. He scrambled to his feet and began to run after her.

On the very first step, one of his feet crossed over the other and pulled him sideways into an uncontrollable spin. He tumbled a surprising distance down the hill before he came to a stop with a painful dive into the dirt.

What was wrong? he wondered. Being clumsy was one thing—he was used to being clumsy—but this was different. He reached over to rub his throbbing backside as he tried to think and gave himself a sharp jab in the middle of the back.

So it wasn't just his feet. He brought his hand forward to see if he could touch his finger to his nose and poked himself in the right eye.

Panicked and in pain, he got up onto his feet and lunged toward Lenora, who was nearing the bottom of the hill. This time, his feet didn't even bother to leave the ground. Before he knew it, he was doing a kind of sideways somersault. He rolled down the hill, picking up speed as he went, and he didn't stop until he crashed with a resounding thwack into an object large enough to halt him.

Unfortunately, that object was Lenora. The two of them fell in a big messy tangle of arms and legs, dust flying everywhere.

"You idiot!" Lenora screamed, beating and kicking at him. "You clumsy oaf! Honestly! Get off me! What is the matter with you!"

He was hopelessly caught in the folds of her gown, and the more he struggled, the more ensnared he became.

"I wish I knew what the matter was," he screamed, "I really do. Ouch! Ouch! Stop it, stop it!" He reached out to push her off and jabbed her in the stomach.

Ouch—this is the last straw, Lenora told herself. She closed her eyes, still biffing away at Coren, and thought, hard. She would imagine him away from her, she would get him off her one way or another.

Nothing. Nothing changed.

"Blast!" she exploded. "I can't do it! I want my powers back!"

"Of course," Coren exclaimed, still desperately trying to ward off her blows and disentangle himself from all that white lace and gauze. "It's my powers. I can't hear the ground, or the trees, or the rocks, I can't orient myself. I'm not used to moving without feeling and hearing everything around me."

"Well, learn!" Lenora ordered as she finally managed to pull her gown away from him, so violently that it ripped.

"I don't have my powers either," she said, impatiently ripping off the piece of fabric that had come loose and tossing it behind her. "But you don't see me becoming a helpless ninny."

Coren could have shriveled up and disappeared right then and there. But he didn't have much time to feel sorry for himself, because floating down the road, skimming just above its smooth white surface, was a long sleek silver object.

A gasp rose up from the crowd approaching the road, and Coren scrambled up, swaying dangerously, to get a better look at it.

"Get out of the way, I can't see," Lenora snapped as she pushed him and he tumbled over again.

Lenora watched with delight as the vehicle came to

a silent stop, hovered for a moment, then settled on the ground. "Ahhh," sighed the crowd, and she along with them. It was like a giant silver cylinder, smooth and gleaming in the sun. A silver door in its side slid silently open and a man jumped out. He was dressed all in red: high red leather boots, red leather pants, a red leather jerkin, and a red helmet. He had an incredibly handsome face, dark and craggy—handsome enough to go with the broad shoulders and thin waist emphasized by the cut of his outfit.

"Welcome to the country of Grag!" the striking fellow said with a bow. "Our leader Hevak welcomes you all! And if everyone would care to climb into this transport, it will be my privilege to take you to our city, many-towered Farren. This way, please."

Without a moment of hesitation, Lenora hurried to the door of the transport—was that what he'd called it? Without pausing or even speaking to one another, the rest of the crowd moved with her.

Coren pulled himself up yet again and carefully tottered behind Lenora, not wanting to go, but definitely not wanting to be left there alone. Three small steps led into the transport, and inside, there was seating for at least a hundred. Lenora raced for a place by the window. Coren pulled himself along by the seat-tops, rushing to make sure he sat beside her. She didn't even look at him as he plopped down next to her.

For that matter, none of the people were looking at

one another. None of them were talking to one another. It was as if they were mesmerized, each in their own private world of awe and admiration. They all shared Lenora's dreamy look of total delight.

Well, Coren thought, it's nice enough, I suppose. The seats were soft, softer than any he had ever imagined. He ought to be enjoying it, but instead he was nervous. Everything was so strange. Where were they? How had they gotten here, really?

When everyone was settled, the vehicle began to move. Coren could feel it lift off the ground and then pick up speed.

"This is amazing, isn't it?" Lenora said, eyes glowing. "Finally some adventure, some excitement! Finally!" She could hardly contain herself.

Well, at least she was talking again, Coren thought. And the rest were beginning to talk too.

They were a motley crew. Looking around the transport, Coren could see every kind of style in clothes and hair. There were long braids, elaborate curls, shaved heads, ringlets, even wigs—worn by both women and men alike. Some of the women were dressed in elegant riding breeches of soft suede, some elaborate lace gowns, some simple dresses. The men had on everything from skimpy tights under long jackets to baggy pants with shirts hanging out or even weird little skirts with socks pulled up to their knees.

Coren was glad he didn't have to wear that! His

skinny legs would look awful in those outfits. He took a surreptitious glance down at his own costume, a pair of tight blue pants and an elaborate and very stiff blue jacket with blue trim over a cream-colored, lace-trimmed shirt. When King Rayden had brought it to him, he'd been astonished at its sumptuous elegance, but now, compared to the others, it seemed almost plain—not to mention very dusty.

He tried to listen in on the conversations around him.

"Yes, indeed, every time I washed my face," he heard the person behind him say, "every time for a week, I saw the same place in the mirror—this place here, as it turned out. I knew I'd end up here soon, it was just a foretelling, as usual, the kind of thing that happens to everybody every day, correct? I've so been looking forward to it actually happening, and now it has!" Then the tone of the voice changed. "It's strange, though—since arriving here, I can't sense the future at all. I mean, I could always feel what was about to happen, of course, just like everybody else. And now I feel nothing. It's gone!"

Coren turned to stare at the speaker. She was a middle-aged woman, elegantly dressed in a long black velvet gown with a neckline so low that Coren blushed and turned away immediately.

Across the aisle from him sat an older man dressed in what looked like a long gown, covered in silver sequins. He was muttering to himself, but he looked fairly harmless.

"Excuse me, sir," Coren heard himself saying, "do you mind if I ask how you got here? Do you know where we are?"

"I am here because I am needed," he replied haughtily. "And I am needed because I am knowledgeable, powerful, special."

This man may have been all those things, but he certainly wasn't modest! "But sir, how did you get here?"

"I'm not sure," the man replied, looking confused for a moment. "But it has something to do with me being special, I know that for sure. And, of course, I wanted a little adventure."

The confused look left him then, and he gazed in wonderment at the scene surrounding him. "And now I have it! What a device this transport is! What a wondrous world! What an adventure this will be! Still, something feels odd, I've been trying to place it—" He shook his head.

Coren said nothing.

"Oh!" he exclaimed. "I know! I haven't composed a poem since we've arrived! That's it. In our land, you see," he said, leaning forward confidentially across the aisle toward Coren, "in our land we compose a poem for every occasion, for every event, for every moment. For instance, my famous words on the birth of King

Jaffray, celebrated throughout the entire land as poem of the week: 'O muse, had I—had I—O muse—' Well, I can't exactly remember it right now. In fact, I can't remember any of my poems—or compose any new ones either. When it comes to verse, my mind is blank! How strange." And he shook his head again and seemed to lose himself in bewildered thought.

So, Coren realized, it wasn't just he and Lenora who had lost their powers. That woman with the embarrassing gown, this poetry man—perhaps everyone on the transport had powers that were now blocked for some reason.

And yes, there was at least one other—a fellow seated farther up the transport in a one-piece, skintight costume. Coren's eyes were drawn to him because he suddenly thrust his arms into the air. He was shouting, "Grow, darn you! Why aren't you growing? It's not natural for arms to always stay the same size. Grow!"

This was getting stranger and stranger by the minute. Coren pulled at Lenora's sleeve to get her attention, anxious to tell her about his discovery. All she did was shake him off.

"Look at it!" she sighed, leaning forward toward the city that was now fast approaching them. "Isn't it magnificent?"

10

Lenora peered out the window, enthralled by the long rows of small dwellings that began to line the streets as they entered the city. The walls of the dwellings were made of bricks of a smooth shiny material and seemed to come in all colors—bright reds, yellows, blues, greens, as cheerful as a child's painting. They were surrounded by elaborate gardens and bushes, exotic plants, and trees hung with vines. It looked like a wonderful place to live, and the people Lenora watched through the window of the transport seemed to think so, too. Small groups of men and women stood in the streets, smiling as they chatted happily with one another, and laughing children were playing tag or skipping rope on the grounds in front of the houses, their brightly colored clothing gleaming in the sparkling sunshine. They all seemed to enjoy one another's company so much. Nobody looked lonely or unhappy. Nobody looked out of place. Nobody looked unhealthy or ugly. Nobody even looked very old.

The buildings grew in size as their journey continued, and Lenora concluded they must be approaching the center of the city. She had to twist her neck to see the tops of some of the buildings—which she assumed were the same towers she'd first seen from the hilltop. They were as magnificent up close as they'd been from afar, covered in ornate statues and balustrades and golden decorations that glinted in the sun. The people who lived here had taste, she decided, there was no question about that.

Finally, the transport rolled into a large square, hovered, and stopped, and the doors slid silently open. Lenora clambered over Coren in her rush to get outside and see what further wonders awaited her.

Left to stumble down the aisle in a crush of other people, Coren made his way to the door, listening to everyone "ooh" and "ah" as they looked through the windows and pointed things out to one another. As far as Coren could tell, they all seemed to have totally forgotten about the various powers they'd lost. Apparently, they were so impressed by this place that none of them could think of anything else.

Or perhaps they just didn't care anymore. Coren heard one fellow, a round-faced, balding man with huge saucer eyes, say, "I do wish my magnifiers were working, don't you? It'd be wonderful to see this fascinating architecture up close. But still, it's beautiful even with standard distance vision. All those statues! So impressive, don't you think?"

Coren was impressed too, sort of. It was all so big.

It made him feel like a small insect. When he finally reached the doors of the transport and looked out, he saw a square large enough to hold tens of thousands of people. And the square was almost filled. It was enough to make any sensible person feel uneasy.

Coren stepped down to the gleaming white pavement, searched for Lenora in the crowd, and then stumbled over toward her as fast as he could manage. By the time he got there, a man was approaching them. He was perhaps a few years older than Coren, but tall, with broad shoulders, curly black hair, blue eyes, and a dazzling smile. He had a long gold earring in his left ear, and the black tights he wore under his short red jacket made it crystal clear that his legs were not the least bit skinny. Lenora, Coren could see, looked like she was going to swoon. The man glanced at her, smiled that ridiculous smile, and invited her and the others from the transport to follow him.

They did. They moved toward the huge crowd in the square, which was standing in orderly rows, a quiet murmur in the air, waiting. Many more transports were lined up beside theirs, but from the way people were dressed Coren guessed that most of those in the square were from the city of Farren itself. They were all wearing those black tights, too.

Coren thought the tights looked a lot more interesting on the women than they did on the men. In fact, he couldn't stop himself from staring at the women. Almost all of them were blond, with their hair piled on their heads. Too thin, Coren thought, but attractive nevertheless—tall, long legs, shapely, very shapely. It was odd, though, how similar they all looked.

And for that matter, how similar all the men looked. There certainly wasn't anybody around with red hair or freckles.

There was a sudden loud blare of trumpets. Turning toward it, Coren saw a building at the far end of the courtyard even bigger than the rest, a huge gleaming white structure covered with gilt statues and ornate balconies. In front of the building was a raised platform, festooned with red and black streamers. A row of trumpeters stood on it, blowing into their instruments. Then two long rows of those red-clad, black-haired men marched out of the white building, into the courtyard, and onto the platform. They were followed by a solitary fellow who looked like all the rest—except he was dressed all in white, with red trim on his uniform and on the cap he wore on his head.

A hush fell over the crowd. The white-clad man stepped up to a podium at the front of the platform. He raised both his arms and stretched them out in a gesture of welcome. His voice, rich and compelling, deep in timbre, flowed out over the audience.

"Greetings!" he called.

"Greetings!" cheered the crowd as one, Lenora

right along with the rest of them. They all rose to their feet, and so did she. They all stretched both arms toward the man in shining white at the podium, and so did she. And she was happy.

She was enjoying herself so much that she hardly had time to be irritated with Coren. He had risen to his feet, stumbling as usual, some moments after everyone else. He seemed to be the only one there without a smile on his face. He's hopeless, Lenora thought.

"Welcome to the newcomers!" the man at the podium called out, his smile dazzling.

As she smiled back, Lenora wondered how she could see his expression. They were quite far back in the crowd, and while she could tell that he was tall and handsome, surely he was too far away for her to make out any details. She must be sensing the smile through his voice, she realized. It seemed to penetrate her very being.

"Welcome to the newcomers," echoed the crowd.

Then they sat, as one. And a moment or so later, Coren sat down too, awkwardly stepping on Lenora's foot in the process. Without withdrawing her eyes from the speaker, she jabbed Coren in the ribs and hissed at him to behave.

"Together, we will build a perfect world," the deep voice intoned. "Together, we will have no wars, no battles, not even a quarrel between two people."

Together, Lenora thought to herself. How wonderful!

"We will live in harmony and happiness," the deep voice shouted.

"Harmony and happiness," Lenora and the crowd echoed joyfully. To Lenora it sounded like a single voice with a single will. No mothers and fathers pushing poor innocent victims around here, she told herself, chanting and soaking up every wonderful word.

"We will live in the brotherhood of man."

"Brotherhood of man."

"We will work and learn together."

"Work and learn together."

"We will rest and play, like children, together."

"Like children, together."

"We are great, together."

"We are great, together."

"We are strong."

"We are strong."

"We are one."

"We are one."

The crowd leaped to its feet again, screaming, "Hevak, Hevak." And the handsome orator lifted his arms above his head once more, to the wild cheers of the crowd. Then he marched off the platform, followed by his troop of red-clad guards.

Lenora found herself on her feet again, clapping. This Hevak, for obviously he was Hevak, was amazing. Just one little speech, a few carefully chosen words, and she knew exactly what he wanted for his world, what she now hoped for, too. She could almost see it: Men and women working together, everyone at peace, harmony and happiness everywhere. It was just the sort of perfect world she might have created for herself, if her parents had ever been sensible enough to allow her to do it.

Coren could see that the glow of ecstatic compliance on Lenora's face was repeated on all the other faces around him, and he was more than a little worried. He wasn't sure what distressed him the most: the fact that they all seemed mesmerized by the orator's words, or the fact that he was the only one left out. Because it certainly looked as if he were the only one who felt nothing when Hevak spoke—nothing but mild irritation at an arrogant man who was conceited beyond belief.

Something strange was going on here, and he didn't like it. He didn't like it at all.

Coren tugged at Lenora's sleeve, trying to get her attention.

"I think we should leave this place, Lenora," he told her.

She shook his hand off her sleeve, hardly even noticing he was there.

"Leave? Why? I love it here. I'm not going anywhere. You can go, if you really want to."

For a brief instant, he imagined himself just grabbing on to Lenora's arm and dragging her out of the square. He could do it, too—if he wanted a couple of broken ribs. Well, what were a few more bruises? He was just about ready to chance it when one of the guards approached. Lenora's breath caught in her throat as her gaze landed adoringly on him.

"You ten in this row," he called out, "would you, please, come with me? Hevak requests it." He flashed a toothy smile.

With a sinking feeling, Coren realized the inevitable: Lenora was going to follow this muscle-bound oaf, without even asking where they were going. And he supposed he'd have to follow along—or be left on his own.

And leave Lenora on her own. It was becoming very clear that Lenora might not be safe by herself. It was as if they were all hearing a secret signal that he couldn't hear. Not that he had any idea about how he could help, but somehow, he couldn't let her go alone. That made him furious with her. "If I ever get out of here," he muttered, "I'll never speak to her again."

"Just follow behind me," the guard announced. "And try to stay together."

The last order was completely unnecessary. As they followed the guard through the dispersing crowd, Lenora and the rest moved in locked step across the gleaming pavement. Coren managed to catch up with them only as they arrived at the bottom of the steps in front of the large white building.

"Now," the man said, turning toward them and smiling yet again, "you are privileged indeed. Step inside for a personal meeting with our leader Hevak."

11

The guard turned toward the huge set of double doors, which suddenly swung open without any action or signal from him, allowing the group to pass into a hall quite different from what Lenora had expected. It was carpeted in shades of purples, reds, and oranges, with designs of trees and flowers. The walls were a rich dark wood that gleamed from the light of the gigantic chandelier above. A burnished wood staircase rose in a spiral from the center of the foyer.

"This way, please."

Lenora and the others followed the guard up the flight of stairs, Lenora's heartbeat quickening at the thought of meeting the great man himself. A thickly carpeted hallway ran either way from the staircase. They walked down the right hallway and through an already open door into a small anteroom. The guard knocked on the inner door.

"Enter."

The guard opened the door and ushered the group in. He quickly organized them into a row in front of Hevak, who sat behind a large desk of polished wood.

Hevak rose, smiling. Lenora thought that he looked even more handsome up close than he had out there on the platform. His gaze moved along the row, and it was clear that he was pleased with what he saw.

But when he looked at Lenora, he gave a visible start. Lenora flushed. Was something wrong with her? It was probably her stupid wedding dress. She'd been so enthralled with her surroundings that she'd forgotten how completely ridiculous she must look.

Slowly Hevak walked around the desk, his gaze still fixed on her. He stopped in front of her and stared right into her eyes.

Lenora stared back, transfixed. His eyes were the deepest blue she had ever seen.

Finally, he blinked and smiled again. And when he smiled at her, he told her how wonderful he thought she was. Not a difficult rebellious child, but a responsible adult, a person with great power and with the wisdom strong enough to use it. A person he could trust.

Then he nodded and broke away from her to go to the next person. She felt desolate.

The strangest part of it, she realized, was that Hevak never actually said a single word to her. He had conveyed everything, telling her how terrific and mature she was, with just a look from his powerful eyes. What a genius!

Standing beside Lenora, Coren was surprised by the intensity of his dislike for everything that was happening. He didn't trust this Hevak. He hated his slick manner and his overdone good looks, and he hated the way Lenora was so obviously mesmerized by the man. All right, maybe he was a little jealous. So what?

As Hevak turned to him, Coren braced himself to remain calm. He knew this man was powerful and there was no use getting into trouble with him unless it was absolutely necessary.

Hevak gave Coren a look very different from the smile he had bestowed on Lenora, a look that made him feel about as welcome as a cobra.

But somehow, he wasn't scared. It just made him curious. Did Hevak dislike him? And if so, why? Coren tried to reach out, ever so tentatively, to see if he could read Hevak's mind. It was almost a reflex, an unconscious act—everything was still silent around him, after all—but he sent his mind out anyway.

Hevak glared at him even more malevolently, and Coren felt an almost physical shove—not to his body, but to his mind.

Suddenly he understood. It was Hevak! He was the one who had shut down Coren's powers—and probably everyone else's, too. Why had he done it?

"Why?" Hevak said, smiling—that is, his mouth smiled but his eyes were hard. "A good question. But just what business is it of yours? Why are you here? You were not called."

Hevak whispered the words into his mind, so that

Coren alone could hear them. Coren felt an excruciating pain in his head. It grew stronger, until it was a pounding, throbbing scream. It was Hevak, it came from Hevak. His eyes drilled into Coren's, pressing, pushing, probing.

It was unbearable. Coren's eyes locked with Hevak's, and he pushed back with all his might, willing Hevak to look away, willing the force to dissipate. His whole body shook with the effort, but it was beginning to work. Ever so slightly, he could feel the force weakening, retreating.

And suddenly he knew what Hevak was thinking.

"No," Hevak hissed, loud enough to pull Lenora out of her daydreams. She turned to see Hevak gazing malevolently into Coren's face.

"No!" Coren cried.

And as Lenora watched in total confusion, Coren disappeared. One moment he was there, and the next he just—wasn't. He was gone.

Smiling triumphantly, Hevak shook his head a little, then turned to Lenora and took her hand in his.

"Don't worry my dear," he reassured her. "He's perfectly safe. It wouldn't suit him here. He didn't like it, did he?"

Lenora shook her head, unable to speak.

"No, I know he didn't." Hevak flashed his winning smile at her. "And you know it, too. His disappearance isn't completely unwelcome to you, is it?"

She could barely breathe. Was that it? Did she want him gone? To be honest, she wasn't even sure anymore. She certainly didn't want to marry him. But she was worried about him—where was he?

And why couldn't she remember his name?

"He's perfectly safe," Hevak repeated. "Perhaps he decided to go back home." Lenora gulped and nodded her head as Hevak gazed piercingly into her eyes. What had she been worried about anyway? There wasn't anything to be worried about.

Hevak blinked, nodded back at Lenora, and then returned to his desk. "And now," he said to them all, "let me tell you why you've been brought here."

Here? There was no here. It was a void—outside of space, outside of time—a place that was no place, a place with no back or forth or up or down. There wasn't even a floor to stand on. Not that it mattered, because it seemed he had no legs left to do the standing—no body at all. Even the freckles were gone. He was nothing but mind, a tangled nest of thoughts and memories floating like a tumbleweed, pulled this way and that by invisible winds through an endless soup of gray, empty nothing. It was very uncomfortable. It was very irritating.

And it was all that greasy monster Hevak's fault, Coren thought. He just willed me out of existence, willed me out of the memories of everybody in that stupid country. It's as if I never was, never existed at all.

And now, Coren could sense, Hevak was erasing him completely. Soon the conceited oaf would totally forget there had ever been a Coren—and Coren would be stuck in this awful soup forever.

But Lenora, surely she hadn't forgotten him so easily?

She had to remember, had to. If only he could enter her thoughts, get her to think of him. Then he'd still exist somewhere, there'd be at least some chance.

Oh please, Lenora, he thought. Think of freckles. Think of skinny legs! Remember me!

Lenora knew she was in the presence of a great man. Despite her nebulous worries about something—or someone, some boy, maybe?—she listened attentively, enthralled by Hevak's compelling, creamy voice. She couldn't help but feel that he was singling her out, looking directly at her and her alone—that she should erase everything and everyone else from her mind.

"You are the chosen," Hevak said, smiling. "I sent a vision to all possible worlds, across the vast reaches of space. I wanted everyone to hear my word, to share my happiness. The strong and powerful of all places and all times received the message, saw the vision. But only the best of those acted on what they heard and were prepared to make the leap between the worlds at the foreordained time. You who understood, and leaped, are the chosen, the only ones in all the worlds intelligent enough to be discontented with the pathetic way things are run in your own lands, the only ones fed up with the ineptness and disorganization and weakmindedness that exists throughout the worlds, whenever the best minds are tied down, restrained by silly rules and laws, made only to protect weaklings from their deserved fate."

How true, Lenora told herself, remembering her parents' silly anger whenever she happened to be brave enough to use the powers she'd been born with. They just couldn't stand knowing that she was stronger than they were.

"When the moment of transit came," Hevak's melodious voice continued, "you heard the call, made the leap between the worlds. You were pulled inexorably by your own wise discontent into my dream. You are the chosen." He smiled warmly, displaying his perfect white teeth.

"But you must act again," he continued. "I have called you here because I have made an important decision. Now that we have perfected this land, it would be heartless to deprive others of our way of life. We have an obligation, a responsibility. We must bring happiness to all people everywhere, in all worlds."

It seemed to Lenora that his unblinking gaze was penetrating to the very heart of her being.

"Go back to your worlds," he said. "Take my dream, our dream, with you. Tell others what you have seen. Show it to them, let them experience it. I will follow and bring you and your people into my fold. Say nothing yet of my arrival. Only show them the wonders. You are my mind. You are me!"

As one, everyone in the room cried in response, "Praise Hevak!" Everyone, including Lenora.

12

As their group was ushered out of the room, a guard standing by the door beckoned Lenora over.

"You have been asked to remain behind," he said. "Our glorious leader Hevak would like to speak to you further." He looked at her in awe, clearly impressed by the honor bestowed on her, then slipped past her through the doorway to lead the others down the corridor.

It was to be a private audience, then! Lenora trembled with excitement as she turned to face Hevak.

He smiled at her. "You don't need to rush back to Gepeth, do you, Lenora?"

He knew her name! He knew her country! But how—?

He must have seen the surprise on her face.

"Oh," he said, "I know everything about my guests. And you, Lenora, you are very special to me. So special that I'd like you to remain here. For a while at least."

Remain? Hadn't he just told them all to return home? It was her duty to do it, wasn't it? And now, he wanted her to stay? "But—but why?" she stuttered.

"Because of who you are," Hevak said, his voice surprisingly fierce. "As I said, you are special, Lenora. Oh, all my guests are special, of course, or else they wouldn't be here at all. But you are like a diamond in a bowl of glass stones."

Lenora swelled with pride. If only her mother and father could hear this great man acknowledge her true value.

"I think you can be of more use here than back home in Gepeth. I need people like you around me, Lenora—people with ideas, energy, strength. Special people. I need you, Lenora." His eyes pierced her own. "If you would do me the honor?"

Lenora's confusion evaporated. She didn't have to go back to Gepeth after all, and staying here, working with Hevak himself was beyond her wildest dreams. Lenora couldn't believe her good luck. "Of course I'll stay!" she exclaimed. "Of course! I love it here!"

"Good!" Hevak nodded, striking the desk in approval. "I have plans for you, great plans. Mellor!" he called.

Another dark-haired young man, clad in red like all the rest, popped his head through the open door.

"Take this young lady to a guest suite in the east wing. She'll be staying with us for a while." Then Hevak winked at Lenora. "For quite a while."

"Yes, sir," Mellor replied, and with a small bow, he ushered Lenora from the room.

Lenora stuttered as she turned to follow. "Thank you, Your—Your Honor, uh, Your Highness. . . ."

Hevak smiled. "My lord will do nicely."

"Thank you, my lord," Lenora said, so excited she could barely contain herself.

Mellor led Lenora out of Hevak's office and through a maze of corridors. He was astonishingly handsome, but nothing compared to the great Hevak. Those eyes of Hevak's, so intense, so compelling. And he thought she was special, an exultant Lenora told herself.

"What is this place called?" Lenora asked Mellor as they moved silently on the thick carpeting, the walls on either side hung with paintings of country scenes.

"Farren Palace," Mellor replied.

Farren Palace—a romantic name for a romantic place. It was perfect.

After a very long walk, Mellor stopped in front of a thick wood door, opened it, and motioned for her to enter.

She gasped when she entered the room. She couldn't have imagined anything better. It was decorated in white and gold. Thick white carpet covered the floors. Two long leather couches were placed in the center of the room, and a gleaming gold chandelier hung over them. There was a large vase filled with flowers on the table between them.

She followed Mellor across the room to another door, which he opened to reveal a separate bedroom. It was done in pale blue, with a round blue chair and table placed near the window, and a four-poster bed draped in velvet in the center. Yet another door in this room revealed a private bathroom, with a huge bathtub all in sand-colored marble in the center and a gleaming gold washstand just beyond it. Heaven.

"It's perfect!" Lenora sighed.

"Of course it is," Mellor said. "An escort will be sent to take you to dinner." He bowed and left.

Back in the bedroom, Lenora wandered over to yet another pair of doors and opened them.

"Oh!" she exclaimed. It was a closet, and it was filled with exquisite clothes—long dresses in velvet and lace, short cotton garments in bold colors, trousers, elaborate silk shirts. And if there was all this here . . .

She ran over to the elaborately carved oak chest of drawers by the bed and began to open the drawers. Snowy white undergarments lay stacked in piles. And filmy stockings in all colors, and jewelry, too, a drawerful of necklaces and earrings glittering in confused piles. It just kept getting better and better.

She ran back to the closet to choose a gown for dinner and noticed at least ten different pairs of footwear—shoes, slippers, boots, even dress slippers covered in sequins. And—could it be? They all seemed to be in her size. She could hardly wait to try them on.

Through the large, arched window, Lenora could see dusk beginning to settle over the gleaming towers of the city. Her stomach started to rumble. Dinner couldn't be that far off. She would bathe in that fancy tub and then change into one of those perfect outfits, she decided.

She put in the plug and turned on the water. She examined some of the many glass bottles on the platform around the tub, opening each one, until she found a rose-scented bubble mixture. This she poured liberally under the hot water as it steamed into the tub. Thankfully, she stripped off her mother's now very bedraggled wedding gown and threw it to the floor.

Seeing it lying there, though, she froze suddenly. Wasn't she supposed to have been married in that? To a boy, yes, but she couldn't quite picture him—her head seemed to go all foggy as soon as she started to think about him. His name was . . . he was . . .

"Coren," he shouted into her mind. "Coren, Coren, Coren! Can't you remember that?!"

And for a moment, she did, but only to want to forget him again. Now she was dismissing him from her thoughts.

And suddenly, he couldn't remember his name.

"Oh, well," Lenora told herself. "That part of my

life is over now. I have more important things to do."
Giving the dust-spattered gown a kick across the room,
she slipped into the tub and sank into the hot, rose-
scented bubbles.

The marble was smooth against her skin as she lay
back and stretched out. She sighed in delight as the
water soothed her sore muscles.

No question about it, she had made the right
choice when she jumped into this place. She picked up
a handful of bubbles and blew them across the room.

And Hevak had chosen her out of all those people
to stay behind. Because she was special. Because she
was strong. She closed her eyes and sighed again.

"I'll just wash up here and then we can have our
dinner."

What? Who—?

Lenora's eyes flew open. Sauntering across the
bathroom, heading for the washstand, was a small person, perhaps half Lenora's height, but clearly full-
grown. In fact, he looked to be around her father's age,
with a touch of gray at the temples. He was dressed in
brown suede pants and a brown sweater.

And she herself was dressed in—nothing.
Absolutely nothing! Thank heavens for all these bubbles, at least. How dare he? She was too startled to
speak.

The little man hurried over to the washstand,
reached up on tiptoes to run some water, and splashed

some on his face. Then he turned around and looked at her. She readied herself for him to see her and race out of the room in embarrassment. But he didn't race out. He just kept right on staring, a look of disgust on his tiny face. Then he called out to the other room. "Drats," he shouted. "There's a big one in the tub. And I wanted a real wash."

Big one indeed! That was the last straw. Lenora began to sputter. "Why—why—how dare you! How dare you! Get out of here this minute!"

"She sees me!" he screamed, his eyes opening wide in terror. "Sumra! Lero! Muni! She sees me!"

"Of course I see you," Lenora exclaimed. "Now get out of my room this instant or I'll—I'll have Hevak himself do something terrible to you!"

He just kept staring at her, his mouth wide open. As Lenora tried to sink further down into the bubbles, three others, just his size, ran into the bathroom. Two females and one male. They all stared at her.

"Just what do you think you're doing?" Lenora shrieked. "Get out of here! Get out! Are you all insane?"

They didn't move. They just stood there, transfixed.

"Can you really see us?" one of the women finally said.

"Yes!" They must be out of their minds, Lenora thought. "I can see you. You can see me. I'm in the tub washing. These are my rooms. I don't want to see you in them. Is that clear? Is that understood?" She finished with almost a shriek.

The little people turned to one another. "She can see us!" they shouted. "It's a miracle, a miracle!"

Lenora had had just about enough. She reached for a thick white towel hanging on a rail attached to the tub and, as she stood up, wrapped it around herself.

"All right," she declared, "that's it. I am not putting up with this nonsense for one more second. You will get out of my rooms or I will throw you out!" She tied the towel tightly around her chest. "Now!"

They didn't move. They just kept staring at her.

"Fine," she said, "fine, if that's the way you want it!" She pulled herself out of the tub and stepped toward them across the shiny marble floor.

Her foot slipped in a puddle, and she felt her legs slide out from beneath her uncontrollably. Then the back of her head crashed against the edge of the tub, and everything went black.

13

She was running, running out of the blackness, tripping, almost falling down the steps of a circular staircase, her head filled with barking noises. The dogs were getting closer, closer, nipping at her heels, a wild blur of pink and blue and green and purple, surrounding her.

"Ouch," she shrieked. "Stop it! Ouch!" But they kept right on nipping. The pink one jumped up on the white towel she had wrapped around her. The towel tore as the dog clawed its way down.

And now they were all over her, clawing, nipping. The towel was in tatters.

"Go away!" she demanded. "Get out of my rooms! I order you to go away!" She suddenly remembered what she had to do. "Dominic, Dominic, Dominic," she shouted.

And poof! The dogs vanished. All but one of them—the white one with the little spots of red fur.

No, it wasn't a dog, after all. It was a boy. Yes, a boy with red hair and freckles, sitting beside her on the stairway and looking into her eyes. She hastily wrapped the shreds of the towel around her.

"Lenora!" he said. "You remember me!"

Of course she remembered him. After all the trouble Prince Coren had caused her, she was hardly likely to forget him. Just what kind of an idiot was he, anyway?

"I thought you were back home," she said to him, remembering what Hevak had told her.

"I wish I were," he said miserably.

"Where are we?" She looked around at the strange scene in confusion.

"Inside your mind, I think. You must be sleeping or something. This is a dream."

A dream? How did Coren get into her dream? Was she just imagining him? Why him, of all people?

"Yes, it must be a dream," Coren was saying, excited. "And here, while you're asleep, your guard is down, and you can remember me. And I can even remember myself. My name is Coren, isn't it?"

Oh, he was really impossible. Couldn't he even remember his own name?

He turned to her urgently. "Lenora," he said, "you've got to help me. I can't leave here without your help. You have to try to remember me—after this, I mean, when you wake up. You have to think about me, or else I'll stop existing altogether."

"Stop existing? Don't be silly. You're back in Gepeth, or Andilla. The real you, I mean. This is just a dream. I'll wake up and you'll be gone."

"That's what I'm afraid of," he exclaimed. "Don't do it, Lenora. Don't leave me here, please don't." Then he moved closer, and grabbed her hand. "It's dangerous for you, too, you know."

Dangerous for her? What could he possibly mean? It made no sense.

"I know it must sound silly," he said, "but Hevak is not what he seems, Lenora."

Hevak, that great leader, that handsome, kindly man, not what he seemed? It was outrageous, it was totally beyond belief. Why was her mind playing these silly tricks on her?

"Why don't you leave me alone?" she wailed, pulling her hand away. Then she willed herself to wake from this nightmare, to make him disappear from her head.

"No, Lenora, no! Don't go. Remember me. Remember me. Remember remember remember . . ." His voice turned into angry barking, hounding her, tormenting her, as the figure of—of some boy or other—disintegrated and turned into gray.

Lenora sat up with a start. Where was she? A terrible pain crashed through her head, and she felt herself being lowered back down. She closed her eyes against the blinding light, then slowly opened them a crack. Little faces hovered over her. She was lying on the four-poster bed. Again she tried to sit up.

"Slowly now, take it easy," the young woman said as they helped her to sit.

"Drink this," the older man said, bringing a small silver cup to Lenora's lips and forcing some of its contents down her throat. It was cold and slightly bitter, and Lenora struggled unsuccessfully to escape the little person's firm grasp. But within seconds, she felt better. The pain settled, the nausea abated. She shook the confused thoughts of skinny, red-haired, yelping dogs out of her head and hardly resisted at all as the little person forced her to finish the cup.

"Better?" the young woman asked.

Lenora nodded.

"Oh, I'm so glad." She smiled, then turned to the little man beside her. "You were right, Lero."

"I told you there'd be medicine in that cabinet," the young man said. "Hevak always provides everything for his guests."

As Lenora's head cleared, she remembered what had just happened to her.

"This is all your fault!" she accused the four anxious faces. "You tramp into the bathroom where I'm lying naked, you stare at me, you go mad just because I can see you, of all things—and—and—"

The older man interrupted her. "Please, let us introduce ourselves and explain."

An explanation was exactly what she needed. She

offered a small, regal nod with her head, giving him permission to continue.

"My name is Peetr," he said with a small bow. "This is my wife, Sumra, my daughter, Muni, and my son, Lero. Sometimes we stay here in the castle, along with many others like us. We come and go as we like, because—well, because no one can see us. That is, no one until you."

"What do you mean no one can see you?" Lenora interrupted. "That's silly! I can see you clear as day."

"But you don't understand," Muni said. "That's what shocked us so much." Muni looked to be a few years older than Lenora, with short black hair, deep brown eyes, and a pretty, dark complexion. Muni's brother had the same black hair and brown eyes as she did and looked to Lenora to be the older of the two. A quick glance at their mother told Lenora where their dark hair and deep brown eyes came from. They all reminded Lenora of someone, but she couldn't think who.

"No, I don't understand," Lenora insisted. "You are speaking gibberish."

"We don't really understand it either," Peetr admitted. "One day we were going off to work, living in our houses, enjoying the company of our friends and families in the evening. We were just like everybody else, normal members of Gragian society. And then, the next day, no one could see us. It was as if we'd suddenly become invisible—everyone below a certain height. And, not seeing us, of course, the others just assumed we weren't there at all. Even our friends started behaving as if we'd never existed."

"Like Angita, for instance," Sumra said. "We went to school together, I was a bridesmaid at her wedding—and all of a sudden, it was like I wasn't there. It hurt, it really hurt."

"It happened to all of us," Peetr said. "And then, big people took over our houses, took over our jobs, took over everything."

"But couldn't you make them realize you were there?" Lenora objected. "Like, punch them or something? If you punched them, they'd have to feel it."

"We tried that," Peetr said. "Believe me, we tried it again and again. We tripped them. We slapped their faces. And yes, we even punched them. But when we did, they just thought they had stomach cramps or something and put it down to food poisoning or a virus sweeping the land."

"We tried throwing things at them too," Muni said. "Lamps, books, even small pieces of furniture."

"But," said Peetr, "all they did was get frightened and run away—they thought we were ghosts, I suppose. Then, later, they'd just return to their homes as if nothing had happened. You have no idea how wearying it is, being ignored like that. How miserable it makes you feel when people treat you as if you don't exist. Finally, we couldn't stand it anymore. We gave up our old homes and left them to the big people. Now we live elsewhere—as far away from the big people as we can manage."

"Unfortunately," Lero added, "we can't leave them altogether. We still have to come into their houses because we need their food, their clothes, their bathtubs! We have none of our own."

"It's not stealing," Sumra hastily interrupted. "We'd pay for it if we could, but we can't. We can't work and earn money to pay for anything!"

This was the wildest story Lenora had ever heard. She shook her head in disbelief.

"You must believe us," Muni said. "It is true. But," her voice was urgent, "you can see us. You're a big person yourself, and yet you can see us! And so it follows that you can help us."

The rest of them all nodded at her.

Lenora looked around the group of little people, uncertain about what to say or do.

"Look," she said finally. "I'd like to believe you, I really would, but I can see you perfectly with my own two eyes."

"Yes," Muni said happily. "You can!"

"And besides," Lenora shrugged, "even if your story were true, what could I do to help?"

The little people looked at one another, clearly uncertain.

Peetr finally replied. "Well, you're staying here in

the guest suite—so you must know our leader Hevak."

"Praise Hevak," the rest murmured.

"Yes, I do know him," Lenora said. "Praise him," she added.

"Perhaps," Peetr suggested, "you could speak to him, tell him about us. If anybody could do something, it's him."

"Yes, Hevak can do anything," said Lero. "Hevak would help us, if only he knew of our plight."

"And he doesn't, you see," said Peetr to Lenora. "We can't speak to him because he can't see us. We've tried writing notes to him and leaving them on his desk, but for some reason, he just crumples them up and throws them away—just like the rest do. I suppose they all think it's a prank of some sort."

Lenora tried to imagine herself telling this wild story about invisible, little people to the mighty Hevak.

"If he really can't see you, and if I did talk to him about it, Hevak would probably think I was crazy," Lenora said. "I would."

Muni took her hand. "Please, just try."

But they could tell from the look on her face that Lenora still wasn't convinced.

"I know," Lero said, "let us prove it to you! Please. Come with us. It'll only take a minute or two."

Lenora took a long look at them. They did seem quite nice, actually. And desperate for her to listen.

She just couldn't say no. And once they realized they couldn't fool her with their crazy story anymore, they'd leave her alone. She hoped.

And if it was true? Well, she'd cross that bridge when she came to it.

"All right," she agreed. "I'll come with you. But get out of here while I dress!"

"Thank you, you won't regret it, thank you." Then they scampered out of her bedroom.

Lenora gingerly got off the bed and onto her feet, glad that her head was almost back to normal. Whatever they had given her to drink certainly was powerful. She examined the contents of the closet. She knew what she wanted to wear for this expedition with the little people—trousers. Princesses weren't allowed to wear trousers back home in Gepeth. Another stupid rule.

She found a pair and felt the fine cotton weave and admired the soft sand color. A rust silk shirt hung beside the trousers, and a pair of short brown boots that laced to the ankle were right beneath them. An entire outfit, all matching! She took everything out, found the appropriate underclothes in the chest of drawers, and was soon admiring herself in the full-length mirror. Oh yes, she definitely liked this country Grag.

After one last satisfied look, she turned and joined the little people in the outer room.

14

"We've decided to take you to the kitchens," Muni said, obviously very excited. "Most of the guests will be in their rooms now, resting, or getting ready for dinner, but the kitchens will be full of workers preparing the meal for tonight."

They hurried down the hallways and then down some back stairs, into a dark corridor. In a few moments, they reached the end of the corridor, and Peetr swung open a pair of double doors leading to a gigantic, smoke-filled, and very hot kitchen. It was filled with people rushing around, carrying things, stirring pots, turning spits. For a moment, they all looked up from their work. Then, seeing strangers—or, Lenora wondered, was it just one stranger they saw?—most of them resumed their tasks. A big woman, wearing a high chef's hat and all dressed in white, hurried over toward them.

"Yes, miss," she said curtly, "what can I do for you?"

"I, I'd just like a little snack," Lenora told her, "for my friends and me."

Lenora could tell the chef was not pleased. "Of

course, miss, anything for Hevak's guests. But as you can see"—she gestured around the room—"we are just a teeny bit busy right now, and if you could wait for a short while, the banquet will begin and dinner will be served."

"My friends are very hungry," Lenora said.

The chef gave Lenora a dark look. "How many, miss?" she said in an icy voice.

"Well, surely you can see," Lenora answered, astonished.

"No, miss," the chef snapped. "Since they haven't come with you, it would be hard for me to see."

It was true then.

"If you are hungry, miss," she said, obviously trying to control her temper, "I'll give you a fresh roll to tide you over until dinner. Surely a nice fresh roll will be enough." The chef didn't notice that Lero was jumping up and down in front of her, wiggling his hands in front of her eyes.

Lenora was convinced, but Muni and Lero must have wanted it to be crystal clear. They raced over to a tray of steaming hot rolls on the counter nearest the door and began to toss them up in the air and juggle them.

"How do you explain that?" Lenora asked the chef, pointing her finger at the rolls flying through the air.

"I don't," the woman replied firmly. "It happens all the time. We just ignore it. That is what Hevak asks us to do and that is what we do. Praise Hevak. And now, if you don't mind, I have a lot of work to do, miss." She thrust a roll into Lenora's hand and turned back to her work.

"Of course," Lenora muttered, and she backed out of the room. Muni and Lero soon followed, munching on hot rolls. Muni gave a roll to each of her parents.

"Now do you believe us?" Peetr asked.

"Yes," Lenora sighed. "I believe you."

"Good," said Muni. "I knew you would."

"We have to get moving," Lero urged. "You have to change for dinner. Because you're going to speak to Hevak for us, aren't you?"

Of course she would. They needed her help. But her heart sank. What if Hevak just thought she was crazy? It would mean the end of his admiration. He might even send her home.

But no, she was being silly. Hevak was good, she was sure of that. He wouldn't just dismiss her. She'd have to make him understand, somehow. And once he knew about the little people, he wouldn't stand by idly and watch their suffering.

"Yes." She nodded. "Of course I'll tell him."

"Good!" Muni exclaimed. "I'll help you choose what to wear."

A few moments later, Lenora was contemplating herself in the mirror, utterly delighted with what she saw. She was wearing a long diaphanous gown, the high neck covered in lace and tiny pearls, the rest flowing layer upon layer of pale blue and mauve. Her slippers were gold, and Muni had done her hair in a braid threaded with gold ribbon. Lenora was pleased. Here she was, dressed in a gown more beautiful than any she'd been able to imagine—and she actually had somewhere to wear it! A banquet! She couldn't wait.

"It fits perfectly," Muni said. "I knew that style would suit you, Lenora." Lenora could see her little face in the mirror, beaming up at her.

Muni was right. It did suit her.

Just then there was a knock on the door.

"Who's there?" Lenora called.

"Beve, at your service," a voice answered. "Hevak has sent me to escort you to the dinner."

Lenora opened the door to find another of Hevak's handsome servants waiting for her. This one was dressed all in black, with a red sash across his chest and another around his waist. He looked dashing indeed, and as he bowed to Lenora, she barely heard Muni say, "We'll wait outside the grand hall. Don't forget us!"

With a smile, Lenora took Beve's arm and let him lead her down the corridors to the center of the palace. They met others on the way, and as each person entered the grand banquet hall, their name was announced.

Lenora was thrilled. She was in a high-ceilinged room with huge arched windows, lit by row upon row of glittering chandeliers. After she and Beve had been announced, they walked down a center aisle, past the long tables festooned with candles and flowers, directly to the front table. There Lenora was seated almost in the center. Her heart pounded. Was she that special? Could it be that Hevak himself might sit in the chair beside her?

Trumpets blared. Everyone in the room rose. They all began to clap. Then Hevak swept into the room, resplendent in white and gold, nodding to everyone but with his eyes always on Lenora.

She wondered if all the others felt the same way. No, it was for her, just for her!

And then, he was there beside her, and he looked her in the eye, bowed low over her hand, and kissed it. Lenora almost swooned.

"Please, my dear, do sit down."

She sank into her chair and gazed at him adoringly. He seemed perfect. He was probably the perfect man.

The dinner flew by in a haze. Hevak chatted with her, asking many questions about Gepeth, which she was glad to answer—she wanted him to know just how awful a place it was compared to the wonders of Grag. He nodded seriously, confirming her opinions, and he asked her question after question. He was so intelligent that he understood the Gepethian customs almost before she finished explaining them, and so wise that he felt just as she did about them.

She did eat, of course, but she really didn't pay much attention to the food. Not with those eyes looking into hers for the entire meal. Then everyone was clapping, and Lenora looked up to see the big woman with the high hat from the kitchen. She wheeled a long trolley into the room and down between the two long tables. She stopped right in front of Lenora and Hevak. On the trolley was a perfect sculpture of a swan. The chef flourished a long stick, then threw something over the swan—and the entire thing burst into flames. These quickly died out, and then, to much loud cheering, she cut the swan into little pieces, which the servants carried to the guests.

Seeing the chef again, Lenora remembered the little people—in the excitement of the banquet they'd gone completely out of her thoughts. As she savored every bite of the deliciously sweet and astonishingly cold dessert that had emerged as if by magic from the flaming swan, she told herself the time had come to keep her promise.

"You know, my lord," she began, "I saw the strangest thing today. Four little people wandered into my room." She gave a little laugh. "It seems I'm the only one around here who can see them! And it bothers them, you know, it really does. And I was wondering if you—"

As she spoke, Hevak's expression changed to a dark frown, then to a glower.

"You should not see them," he roared. "Only I— only I should—only I can—!" For a moment he looked quite bewildered. Then he jumped to his feet and shouted out, "Take her away! She is dangerous! She is a danger to my person! Away with her!"

"No!" Lenora cried. "What are you doing? I'm not a danger to you. Stop!" But already, two strong guards had grabbed her arms and were lifting her bodily from the chair. "Let go of me! My lord, I could never be a threat to you," she pleaded. "I'm devoted to you, really!"

Hevak turned his face from her, and the guards lifted her up and dragged her away from the table. "Someone help me!" she screamed. "Stop this. I don't know what I've done!" And then, much to her surprise, "I want my mother! I want my father! You can't do this to me! You'll be sorry!"

They hauled her screaming all the way to the door and out into the corridor, where Muni and Lero stood, horrified expressions on their faces.

"You!" she shouted at them. "This is all your fault. Get away from me, get away, get away, get away!" She was so angry that she tried to kick at both Muni and Lero, but it was futile—the guards had already dragged her out of range.

"It's not our fault," Muni said as she ran after her.

"Who is she talking to?" one of the guards said.

"Beats me," the other replied. "She must be some nutcase Hevak needs to get rid of. Talking to thin air."

Lenora decided it might be wise not to say anything for a while. She clenched her jaw and let herself be dragged. Down the stairs they went, over the thick carpets, then down more staircases of plain wood, until Lenora thought they could go no lower. Soon the smells around them became distinctly unpleasant. The wood was replaced by stone floors and stone walls dripping with damp. Lenora held her silence until she saw a disgusting little animal scurrying down the hallway. Then she screamed.

"Let me go!" she pleaded. "There's been some terrible mistake. Please. Just let me talk to Hevak. Just let me explain."

The guards ignored her. Finally, they reached an open door, stopped, threw her in, and slammed the door shut behind her.

Lenora turned and beat on the door. "Let me out! Let me out!" She was furious! How dare they treat her this way?

And she was afraid. What was that horrid little animal with a sharp face and long tail that had run in front of her? Were there any more of those awful things here in this room? She turned but could see nothing except black. Black everywhere.

"Let me out!" she screamed again. And then she began to cry. "I want to go home," she sobbed. "I hate this place. How dare they treat me like this!"

15

As her eyes adjusted to the dark, Lenora looked at her surroundings. From the small bit of light that came in from the cracks around the door, she could dimly make out a tiny room. There was no window, no bed or table or chair. Just the floor, the walls, the awful sewerlike smell, and her.

Or at least she hoped she was alone. Who knew what creepy little things might be hiding in that murky gloom, all set to scoot across the floor and—

She didn't even want to think about it.

Well, this was a fine mess. Hevak had seemed so kind, so wonderful. And then he was ranting and raving like a banshee. It was certainly worse than any tantrum she'd ever had.

And he'd had the nerve, the utter gall, to have her picked up like a sack of potatoes by those big ugly brutes of his and unceremoniously dumped into this horrid, dank hole. As if she were some common criminal—she, Lenora, the Princess of Gepeth!

How dare he? How could he? Well, he wasn't what

he seemed, that was certain, for all his wavy hair and pearly teeth and big ideas. No, he was nothing but a big bully who pushed everybody around and then exploded if he didn't get his own stupid way. She hated him. Loathed and despised him. How could she ever have felt otherwise?

Well, she had herself to blame. She'd been warned, after all. "He's not what he seems, Lenora"—she clearly remembered someone saying that to her. Why hadn't she listened? Whoever said it was right.

But who was it? Who had said it, and when?

Ah, it was coming back now—amazing how anger helped you to think more clearly. It was in a dream. Yes, in the bathroom, after she fell and got knocked out, she'd dreamed of a stairway—and a boy. He'd warned her about Hevak, and she had been furious with him and dismissed him from her mind.

It was a boy she knew, a boy she remembered knowing, once. Yes, a boy with cute freckles and interesting red hair. Coren! That was his name. He had asked her to remember him.

Suddenly she remembered him perfectly. She could see his face in her mind as clearly as if he were standing there before her.

That was odd. How could she have forgotten him so totally, so completely? And then she gasped and put her hand to her mouth.

Hevak! Of course. Back there, in Hevak's office—

Hevak had done something, and Coren had disappeared, right before her eyes.

Is that what had happened to the little people? Could Hevak actually make people disappear? Was it possible?

Some words of her mother's echoed in her mind. "You've imagined some silly world where your own dear, sweet mother doesn't even exist." Of course it was possible.

And for some reason, Hevak had done it to an entire people. Or almost done it, it seemed, for somehow, she still knew they existed even if no one else did.

Perhaps he had done something like that to Coren. Yes, Hevak had obviously lied to her. Coren wasn't back home at all. He was probably floating around in some gray place, like the one her mother had told her about.

Poor Coren. He'd be terrified of a place like that. She could see him clearly in her mind now, sitting on a stair, looking at her pleadingly and saying, "Don't leave me here, please don't!"

As if there were anything she could do about it now. But she couldn't, of course. Hevak had blocked her powers.

It made her angry. If it wasn't for Hevak, she'd have Coren out of that gray place and back this very instant, right here in this very spot where she could look after him and keep him out of trouble.

Oof. All the air rushed out of her lungs, and she felt herself crushed by a heavy weight.

The ceiling was falling in, the whole place was caving in on her, she thought in a panic. She beat against the heavy weight with all her might, trying to get some space to breathe.

"Oof! Ouch! Ooh!" Now the ceiling was talking! "Ouch! Ouch!" it was saying. "Stop it, Lenora, stop it!" And now it was hitting back at her.

It wasn't the ceiling, after all. It was a person. Someone had suddenly appeared out of nowhere and landed on her like a ton of bricks and nearly killed her.

It was him, of course—Coren.

"You bumbling fool! Honestly! Get off me! What is the matter with you!" She jabbed him again.

"Ouch! That hurts! I'll get off, Lenora, if you let go of me. Ouch!" Coren said.

With one last little jab, she pulled herself free. Unfortunately, her wonderful banquet gown ripped in the process. Yet another dress ruined!

And then it hit her. He was back! She had wanted Coren back, and he'd come back!

"Coren!" she shouted in wild excitement. "I did it! I brought you back!"

Without even realizing what she was doing, she reached over, pulled him toward her in a huge bear hug, and planted a kiss right on his lips.

Even more astonishing, he kissed her right back. A

rather good kiss, too, she had to admit. Not that she had anything to compare it with—it was her first real kiss—but it was much better than anything she'd expected from him, much better even than anything she'd imagined. She kept her arms folded tightly around him and waited for another.

"Good heavens," he said, breaking from her grasp and taking in their murky surroundings. "Where on earth are we?"

16

"We're in some kind of jail, in the basement of Hevak's castle," Lenora grumbled, irritated at having to admit how much trouble she'd landed herself in.

"What are we doing here?" Coren asked, totally bewildered.

"It's all because of these little people I met," Lenora said, the vexation clear in her voice. "You see, they're invisible."

"What?"

"I can see them perfectly, but apparently, nobody else can. They're invisible to everyone but me."

"Oh," said Coren, confused.

Lenora didn't notice. "So," she continued, "I decided to tell Hevak about them. About the little people, I mean. That was a big mistake, because for some reason, he was furious with me! He said something about me being dangerous—me, of all people!" Her voice shook with emotion. "How could anybody think I was dangerous?"

For some reason, Coren didn't answer.

"And then," she continued, "he threw me down

here! He had his guards drag me down here like a sack of potatoes. There are disgusting rodents down here!"

"Hevak!" Coren said, his voice grim in the darkness. "I should have known. He's the dangerous one."

"I know. You should have seen his face."

"I can imagine it. In fact, I don't even have to imagine it. I saw it myself, back there in his office when he made me disappear like that. It was awful."

"But why? Why did he do it?"

"Because he didn't want me here. I wasn't supposed to come in the first place. And just before he made me disappear I discovered that he controls everything here. He's the one who took away our powers, everyone's powers. He controls how people act, what they can do, everything. In fact, once he got rid of me I think he must have forgotten about me. He must have, or I never could have gotten through to you just now and gotten back here."

"Gotten through?" Lenora said, puzzled. "But I brought you back here. It was me, not you. I imagined you here, and here you are!" Then she realized he didn't know yet—that's why he was so confused. "You see," she said happily, "I have my power back!"

There was silence for a moment. "Uh . . . well, no, you don't, Lenora. It's me. I'm the one who has my power back."

"What do you mean? I clearly remember thinking you—"

"It was me doing it, not you. That's why you suddenly remembered me. It was me, inside your head. You see," he explained patiently, "when you started to think of me, I was able to enter your thoughts. And once you completely remembered me, I just reappeared automatically, because Hevak's disappearing trick can't work as long as someone remembers you!"

"Never mind Hevak," Lenora said, her eyes narrowing. "Do you actually mean to say that you came into my thoughts totally uninvited? Is that what you're telling me?"

"What was I supposed to do? You'd completely forgotten me. I was stuck out there in this gray nothing. It was horrible. I could have been there forever!"

"That's no excuse!" Lenora snapped. "There are worse things than hanging around in the gray—like invading a person's mind, for instance!"

"You've got to be joking!" he spat out. "Why, that's the most selfish thing I've ever heard! That's what comes of living in a country where no one can enter anyone else's thoughts. You have no sympathy for anyone else because you have no idea how they feel! You're just a spoiled brat!"

A spoiled brat? "How dare you!" she exclaimed. How dare he get mad at all? A meek apology would be more in character. That experience in the gray had definitely had an effect on him.

She sat and thought about it for a moment. Then,

suddenly, she reached out and jabbed him.

He clutched his stomach. She'd acted so quickly that he hadn't even caught her thinking about it. "Why did you do that?"

"To see if it would hurt. And it did. So, you're really there. You're not just a figment of my imagination."

"Of course I'm not, I just said that."

"Well, then, think about what you're saying. Your people can read thoughts and make one another imagine that things are real—but you still know they're just thoughts, correct?"

"Yes. So?"

"So it's me who can really turn my thoughts into reality. If you're real enough to feel pain, then I must have my powers back. So there!" *And he thinks he's so smart,* she added to herself.

"Well, I'm certainly not as stupid as you think," he shot back. "It was me that brought me back, not you."

"Get out of my mind, you—you—"

For a long, tense moment, there was silence. "You make me so mad," Lenora finally said. "I wish you were at the bottom of a deep lake."

All at once, Coren wasn't there anymore.

"Oh!" Lenora said. Well, at least he'd have to believe her now. She wished him back again, but across the room. He'd barreled into her one too many times already.

Coren was dripping wet and coughing up fishy-tasting lake water. "I give up," he said morosely in between coughs. "You have your powers back. We both have our powers back."

Finally he believed her. Lenora moved over to him and gave him some good stiff blows on the back to get the water up. "Now that we have them, we have to figure out how to use them to get out of this place."

"We could just go home," Coren suggested, hopefully.

"No, I promised those little people I'd help them. I can't desert them now. Still, I think I'll imagine us out of this horrible place. Let us be—oh, I suppose, standing in the corridor just on the other side of this door."

"Don't, Lenora!" Coren shouted, leaping to grab her and spraying her with fishy water. "There's a guard out there, a really big one. I can sense his thoughts, he's armed, he'll—"

But it was too late. She had already closed her eyes and willed it to happen.

And opened them onto the darkness of the cell.

"It didn't work," she cried. "Why didn't it work?"

"It's a good thing it didn't work," said Coren, shaking his arms and legs to get rid of some of the water and spraying her yet again. "You could have gotten us killed. Just let me think." He paused. "This must have something to do with Hevak. Perhaps Hevak can only control what he knows. But he can't know everything, and he can't control what he doesn't know."

"I don't understand."

"It's perfectly logical. He's forgotten all about me. I don't exist for him. And since he knows nothing about me, I have my powers back. He can't block whats he doesn't know is there."

"I suppose that would be true. But what about me? Why can I do some things but not others?"

"You can do what he doesn't know about! He didn't know about me being here, so he couldn't control you sending me to that stupid lake and nearly drowning me—honestly, Lenora! I'm still soaking."

"I said I was sorry."

"But Hevak does know about this prison, so you can't change it. And he wants you to be in it, so you can't imagine yourself out of it."

"Well—it makes sense. Yes," she conceded, "you're probably right." And she couldn't help but admire his thinking. "But what can we do then? How can we get out of here?"

"There has to be a way," Coren said.

As if in answer to his request, a beam of light pierced the gloom and the small square window in the door opened.

"Are you all right, Lenora?" a voice whispered.

It was Muni. Lenora could see the top of her head through the small bars in the window.

"You! It's your fault I got stuck in this awful place."

"I'm sorry, Lenora," Muni said. "We all are. You

have to believe me, we never imagined anything like that would happen. At any rate, we've come to get you out. We've arranged a diversion. A rather good one, too. Right about now"—she turned toward where the guard must be standing—"yes, right about now, that guard is going to suddenly find himself in a sticky situation." And she stared to giggle.

A surprised shout blotted out her laughter. "Aagh!" the guard shrieked. "What is that? What's happening? Ooh," he wailed, "get off me, get off me, get—ugh!" Then his screams became muffled, as if his mouth had suddenly filled up with something.

"He's gone," Muni said triumphantly, turning back toward the window again. Then Lenora and Coren heard the key in the door, and it swung open to reveal Muni and Lero standing there, Muni perched on Lero's shoulders.

"Good work, Father!" Muni shouted down the corridor as she jumped down to the ground. "It'll take that big lug awhile to get that stuff off him!" She turned back toward the cell. "Let's go."

Lenora stepped through the door first. She could see Peetr and Sumra standing at the end of the hall, both grinning. Each was holding an almost empty jar of honey.

"We dumped it over his head!" said Peetr as he noticed her puzzled face.

"Simple but sweet," said Sumra.

Peetr laughed. "No time to waste," he chided. "Let's hurry." Suddenly he noticed Coren and paled. "Who's that?"

"He can see you, too," Lenora said. "Can't you, Coren?"

"Why, yes," Coren said, "of course. Why shouldn't I see them?"

"Who are you?" Lero asked.

"My name is Coren. Prince Coren of Andilla. I came here to this land with Princess Lenora, and then Hevak got rid of me by imagining me out of existence."

"And," Lenora said, "I'm sure he did it to your people, too, and that's why you're invisible to everybody. Don't you think so, Coren?"

"I don't know," Coren mused. "After all, these people are still here. But I was floating around in that gray place, where I couldn't even remember my own name. No, it's not the same. Still, it was Hevak who did it— that's one thing we can be sure of."

"Hevak?" Peetr was astonished.

"That isn't possible!" Lero added.

"Hevak is good," Sumra said with great assurance. "It couldn't be him."

"Praise Hevak," the little people all murmured.

"But—" a look of horror spread across Muni's face—"it had to be him. He controls everything. Why didn't we think of that before?"

"Probably because he didn't want you to," said Lenora ruefully, remembering how she herself had forgotten Coren.

The little people were clearly stunned by the idea. They stood there in shock, unable to move.

"Could we, perhaps, discuss this later?" Coren said anxiously. "When Hevak and his entire castle aren't after us, for instance?"

"You're right," Lenora said. "Let's go." She moved swiftly off down the corridor.

Furious that she'd started off without even thinking about where she was going, Coren rushed after her. The little people followed, still in a daze. Muni, who seemed a little less bewildered than the other members of her family, overtook Lenora and then led the way as the group crept up the stairs. She was about to turn to her left when Coren put a hand on her shoulder.

"Don't go down there," Coren whispered. "Some of Hevak's people are coming toward us."

"How do you know?" Peetr asked as he trotted up behind Coren.

"I can sense their minds," Coren replied. "I'm reaching out, trying to feel if anyone is around."

"That's ridiculous," Muni said, moving forward. "Nobody can—" But she stopped suddenly and scurried quickly back, making a gesture with her hand to stop Coren and Lenora. "You're right," she whispered, looking at Coren in awe. "They are there. If we'd gone that way, they would have seen you two for sure. How did you do that?"

"It's just this gift I have," Coren whispered back. He paused for a moment, as if listening, and then pointed. "That way is clear. Does it lead to an exit?"

Peetr nodded. They all hurried down the corridor, up another flight of stairs, down another corridor. Finally, they saw a large door ahead of them.

"Hurry," Coren urged, "I can feel them, many of them. Big brutes, too. Not far away now. And they're really upset—they've discovered our escape!"

The group slipped through the door, which opened on to the grounds behind the palace, and quickly shut it behind them. They stopped for a moment to get their bearings.

As she caught her breath, Lenora noticed Coren staring at her, his mouth slightly open.

"You look like a fish!" she declared. "What are you gaping at?"

"You," he said, still staring at her. He turned beet red and glanced at the ground. "That's a lovely dress," he mumbled.

Lenora felt herself flush, too. "Well," she finally managed to get out. "Yes, it was lovely, before somebody ripped it. But this isn't exactly the time to be admiring a new fashion."

"It wasn't the fashion I was admiring," Coren muttered. Then he started.

"They're right behind us!" he said. "Just behind that door!"

17

The group surveyed their surroundings. By now it was night and the sky was dark, but the scene before them was lit by many tall lamps, and Lenora could see a huge park stretching ahead, filled with ornate flower beds, shrubs, trees in blossom, and lush green grass cropped close. There were people strolling around, and others riding sweet little ponies, quietly cantering up and down the pathways.

"If we can just get through the park and into the city streets," Muni said, "we can lose them. I know the city like a mother knows her baby's face!"

"Let's get those ponies!" Lenora shouted, and raced toward one of them.

"Wait, Lenora, wait!" Coren shouted after her. "There are people riding them!"

Lenora ran toward a young man sitting astride one of the ponies. "Hey, you with the hat," she called, "come here! I have to tell you something." He turned the pony toward her, and when he bent over, she yanked his hair and pulled until he came right out of the saddle and landed on the ground, too amazed to say or do anything. Laughing, she leaped up on the pony and dug her heels into its flanks, pulled on the pony's reins, turned, galloped back, and scooped up an utterly astonished Muni into the saddle in front of her.

Coren took a deep breath. How could she? Well, he wasn't going to do that.

But he had to get out of here somehow. He ran over to a young woman on a pony, then paused, bowed, and said, "Please, miss, my sister is in terrible trouble; it's an illness of some sort!" He pointed at Lenora, who was galloping wildly away and toppling over anyone who got in her path. "Look how she's behaving! Could I borrow your pony to go after her?"

The young woman smiled sympathetically. "Poor dear. Of course you can have the pony." She leaped lightly off, and Coren politely thanked her as he mounted. Then he turned back to the little people still standing by the door.

"Never mind us," Peetr said. "We'll just walk. No one can see us!"

"Who cares," Lero shouted, "I want a ride! Wait!" And he rushed over and vaulted onto the pony.

As he threw his arms around Coren's waist, a mob of guards burst from the palace. They saw Lenora galloping away, and one of them began to shout, "Get the transports, we'll run them down from the air."

"Go to the underground warrens," Peetr yelled to Coren and Lero. "They can't track you there!"

"Yes, Father," Lero called back. "We'll meet you there!" Then he yelled into Coren's ear. "You smell like fish! And why are you so wet?"

"It's a long story," Coren shouted back over his shoulder as he spurred his pony. Soon they were galloping in close pursuit of Lenora. As they raced along, Lero called ahead to Muni. "Head for the warrens!"

"Keep to the pathways," Muni advised Lenora, hanging on for dear life. "It's true everyone can see you, but it's faster than going through the trees. We just have to get across this park before they manage to get their transports to us. Once we're in the city we can lose them."

Lenora, her hair quickly coming loose from its braid and whipping around her face, grinned despite herself. She knew she was in danger, but barreling through the park, the wind on her face, the speed—it was fun. She glanced back to see Coren, a determined grimace on his face, trying to keep up with her.

"She has no fear," Coren grumbled.

"What?" said Lero.

"She has no fear," Coren repeated louder. "Lenora. She's reckless."

"I would admire her for that," Lero said.

"I do," Coren admitted. "But she's dangerous to be around!"

"Pooh," Lero replied. "What's life without adventure?"

"Calm," Coren answered. "Life is calm without adventure."

"Yes—and boring!" Lero declared.

"Well, yes," sighed Coren. "Boring sounds very good to me right now."

Lero laughed. "You don't mean that!"

"Don't I?" Much to his surprise, Coren wasn't sure. He seemed to be feeling so different, now that he was no longer in the gray. And acting differently, too. Why, he'd even kissed Lenora when she grabbed him—kissed her right back without even thinking. And enjoyed it. Not that he had anything to compare it with, it being his first real kiss.

He took a quick glance back down the path. Some of the guards had also taken ponies and were following them, but they were still a good distance behind.

Then, he heard a loud noise overhead, like a million bees swarming at once. A chill ran down his spine.

"Engines," Lero shouted. "Transport engines. Hevak has a landing surface for flying transports right on top of the palace. They'll soon be airborne!"

"Wonderful," Coren exclaimed, "flying transports!" The mere sound of them was scary. "How much farther?"

"Not much," Lero assured him.

"Turn off this path," Muni ordered Lenora. "We'll leave the ponies here."

Lenora did as requested. They waited impatiently for Coren and Lero. When the two young men joined them, Muni and Lero took the lead.

"Don't forget, no one can see us," Muni said. "So you two just walk quickly as if you know where you're going. The streets won't be busy now anyway."

The group hurried out of the park and into the street lit only by pale lamps. They all felt safer away from the bright light of the park.

"This way," motioned Lero as he opened the door to a large square building. Just inside was a set of steps. They hurried down into a long corridor that curved off into the distance, with doors opening on to it all along the way.

"Where are we?" Lenora asked.

"This corridor connects almost all the buildings in the city," Muni said.

"But this is just the top layer," Lero added. "It soon starts circling downward. If we can get to the lower level without being detected, we'll be safe."

"Safe for the moment," Coren cautioned.

Lenora looked at him and rolled her eyes.

"Well, that's better than the alternative," she said as she strode briskly forward.

18

As they spiraled their way down the curving corridor, ever lower and lower, Coren sent his mind out, trying to catch the thoughts of their pursuers. Every once in a while he could sense guards on the ground overhead, but so far it seemed they hadn't thought of looking underground.

He was also catching random thoughts of the people who lived above. Those thoughts he found troubling—they were so ordered, so controlled. Everyone he overheard was concentrating strictly on performing tasks. There were no flights of fancy, no children imagining monsters or wonderful creatures, no adults telling stories. They might as well be machines, he thought, like those transports they have.

"What are these corridors for?" Lenora asked. They were clean and gleaming white and lit by a soft glow. Nobody else was in them, and after a little while there were no longer doors opening off them.

"Well," Lero replied, "this is the oldest part of Farren City. The story goes that in his younger years Hevak built this as a play area. He created teams that tried to outsmart one another in an elaborate game of hide and seek."

"Does he still use it?" asked Coren.

"No," Muni replied, "he doesn't. After a while, apparently, he won the game too easily and got bored with it."

"Anyway," Lero continued, "he seems to have forgotten all about it. We've never seen him or anyone else down here."

That was all the conversation they had during the whole trip. They walked quickly—ran, too, whenever they could—and had little energy left for talking. The circles gradually grew tighter and tighter, and the corridor sloped more and more, until they felt like they were walking down a hill.

"Almost there," Muni panted, and Lenora saw a rounded arch ahead of them.

They stepped through the arch, and both Lenora and Coren stopped and gasped. Beneath and above them, a huge cave stretched almost as far as their eyes could see.

"It's enormous," Lenora said.

"It's amazing the city doesn't fall into it," Coren observed.

"Anything is possible for Hevak," Lero said. It wasn't clear whether he admired Hevak now or despised him.

The cave stretched back, revealing an area almost

as large as the entire grounds that surrounded Lenora's home in Gepeth. But it wasn't just one big cave, it was full of strange rock formations that broke it up into a multitude of smaller units.

As they looked more closely, Lenora and Coren could see that each of these pockets was full of people. Little people.

Muni and Lero laughed as Lenora and Coren gaped in amazement at the tiny multitude below them.

"Didn't know there were so many of us, did you?" said Lero.

"Most of our people live here," Muni explained, "because we got sick of being reminded all the time that we don't really exist. In small doses, it's bearable— but not as a steady diet. Here, among ourselves, we're as real as you are."

Lenora looked down at the busy scene beneath her in wonder. Each small unit looked cozy and warm. Multicolored thick rugs covered the stone floors. Thick patterned cushions were strewn everywhere. There was a soft glow of light over everything.

"Do the lights ever go off?" Coren asked.

"No," explained Muni. "There's no day or night here. Only this."

"I think Hevak must have forgotten about this place at some moment when the lights were on," said Lero.

Just then Peetr and Sumra came up behind them,

puffing, Peetr clutching his side from running too fast.

"Ah, thank goodness," he panted, "you've arrived safely. Please follow us to our little home."

Coren and Lenora followed Peetr as he made his way down from the ledge, through a maze of rock and staring eyes. A hush fell on the little people as Lenora and Coren passed. The two of them were obviously big people. What were they doing down here?

"Now we must plan," Peetr said as they settled down on some soft cushions in a relatively private enclave. "Lenora, you are obviously in danger, and I assume your young friend is as well. How can we help one another?"

Lenora thought for a moment. "What I can't understand," she said, "is why you and your people are in this strange state. In between, I mean, here but not here. When Hevak wanted to get rid of Coren he just got rid of him. Totally."

"Perhaps," Coren suggested, "it takes a long time for an entire people to completely forget another entire people. I was just one person, after all, and hardly anybody here even knew me, but you and your people"—he turned to Peetr—"everyone knew you, knew about you. Some were your friends, weren't they?"

The little people nodded.

"It would take a lot of work to erase you from all those people's minds. But once it's obvious to Hevak that no one sees or remembers you anymore, he'll be able to send you all into the gray, too."

It was clear from the expression on their faces that the thought terrified the little people.

"Well," Lenora said in a determined voice, "we certainly can't let him disappear you altogether. I won't have it. We have to stop him."

"But how?" Sumra sighed. "He's so powerful!"

"Don't worry, Mother," Lero said, draping his arm over Sumra's trembling shoulder. "We'll find a way. We will—won't we?"

Lero addressed his question to Lenora, but it was Coren who answered.

"I think I've discovered something that could help," he said slowly. "It's something in your minds."

Muni frowned and turned to him. "You entered our minds?"

"Yes," said Coren, "and—"

"I don't like that," Muni objected. "Not at all. Surely you should have asked first?"

Coren suddenly looked quite sheepish and turned red in the face. Lenora couldn't help herself. She burst out laughing. Coren shot her an angry glance.

"It's hard not to hear things sometimes," he said.

"That's no excuse," said Peetr.

"No excuse at all," said Muni.

"If you want my opinion," Lenora said, suppressing a giggle, "I think you're being too hard on him."

"But you get furious when I do it to you!" Coren said.

"That's different," Lenora said. "If this is something that can help, none of us can afford to be too sensitive."

Coren shook his head. He would never understand her.

"So what did you find?" Lenora asked.

"Lenora is right," Muni conceded. "Tell us what it is, Coren."

"Trolls," Coren replied.

"Trolls!" exclaimed all five of his companions at once. They looked at him as if he had taken leave of his senses.

"Yes, trolls! Short stocky people with frizzy hair and sharp teeth. Some of them have more than one head. I believe they used to live here, in Grag, just as you do," he said to the little people, "because they're stored clearly in your minds."

"Well of course they are," said Sumra. "Everyone knows about trolls, but they're just imaginary, storybook creatures."

"No," Coren objected, "they're not. The trolls I see in your minds don't feel like storybook creatures. They're real. They—well, they smell. Really bad. I think Hevak sent these trolls off to the gray—and I think we should bring them back."

"But why?" Lenora asked, intrigued. "What would we accomplish by bringing them back?"

"I'm not sure, really, except that I assume Hevak didn't want them here. He had a reason for getting rid of them. They must be some kind of threat to his power."

"Yes," Lenora mused. "It makes sense. Even all of us being here and knowing we all exist defies his control, right? Well, the more the merrier."

"That's what I was thinking," Coren said. "At any rate, we have a responsibility, don't we? I mean, once we know they're there, we can't just leave them there."

"Of course not," Lenora said. "And besides," she added, rubbing her hands, "it sounds like fun!"

The little people looked horrified.

"Trolls are disgusting!" Muni said.

"They're cruel and dangerous!" Sumra warned.

"They're not trustworthy!" Peetr added.

"Now I know for certain that those trolls once existed," Coren said, "because if they didn't, why are you getting so upset about them?"

It was a good question. The little people looked at one another in confusion.

"And besides," Coren continued, "all that about the trolls being disgusting, deep down in your thoughts you know it isn't true. They're not cruel at all. Deep down, you like trolls." He stopped a moment to capture a thought. "Hulder, for instance. Yes, Hulder, she was a friend once, Sumra! Your best friend! And, and, a bridesmaid at your wedding! Wasn't she?"

"Hulder? She couldn't—I wouldn't—I—" Sumra looked very confused.

"Hevak must have planted those thoughts in your brain," Coren continued. "Made you think of trolls as disgusting and smelly."

"Oh, it's all nonsense," Peetr said impatiently. "How do we know these imaginary trolls would even be willing to help us?"

"They'd help," Lenora said. "They'd know they have to help defeat Hevak or they'll end up back in the gray."

"She has a point," Lero remarked. "And it's worth a try, at least."

He looked eagerly at Peetr who, in turn, looked at Sumra. She was muttering to herself. "Hulder? Did I know a Hulder?"

"Good," said Lenora briskly, smiling at the little people, "then it's settled. What do we do, Coren?"

"To bring all those trolls back, we'll need everyone's help," Coren said. "All your people, Peetr. They're going to have to think about trolls as hard as they can."

"I'll go speak to them," Peetr said.

As he and his family went off to gather the others, Coren told Lenora his plan to get the trolls back.

"I'll try to make the little people conscious of the trolls hidden in their memories," he said, "and then you can just make them real. It should be quite simple."

As it turned out, though, getting the little people to think about trolls wasn't going to be as easy as it sounded. When Peetr had gathered them all together into a large meeting place in the center of the cave and told them what had happened to Lenora and what Coren had seen in their minds, they just laughed.

"Oh, sure, trolls," said a fellow in the front row. "As if our glorious leader Hevak would allow ugly things like that in his country!"

"And besides," added another, "nobody can read thoughts. That's just a fantasy." Those around him chortled gleefully.

Peetr turned to Coren. "I was worried this might happen," he said. "You'd better get busy and do whatever it is you're going to do, because they won't hang around here much longer."

Coren gazed out at the multitude of laughing, skeptical little faces and shook his head. "It won't work if they don't believe," he sighed.

"Oh, stop that," Lenora snapped. "All you have to do is gain their confidence. I know!" She leaned over and whispered into his ear.

"That might do it." He nodded. "I'll give it a try."

"I'll get their attention for you." Lenora turned to the crowd, who were still laughing and hooting. "Quiet!" she shouted, in a voice so loud it cut right through the din and brought immediate silence. "Now listen. Prince Coren of Andilla has something to say."

Coren had his eyes closed. Suddenly he opened them and announced, "You're right, Murno," and he turned toward an old man near the front. "I was born with these red spots on my face. They're not a rash."

Murno started, astonished to have his private thoughts revealed in this way.

"And yes, Avila," he went on with growing confidence, "I do know that, but you have nothing to worry about. I won't tell a living soul. I promise you, your secret is safe with me."

The little woman named Avila blushed a deep red.

"And you, Dravilla, stop worrying about where your young Arfa is. He's just over there behind that rock, watching some ants and thinking about what he'd like for a bedtime snack. Dried apricots on toast."

This last bit of information persuaded the entire assembly, for it seemed young Arfa had a reputation for thinking about food all the time, and a passion for dried apricots.

"Good," said Lenora as she watched the crowd buzz in astonishment. "I knew that would work." Then she shouted for silence again.

"Now that you know Prince Coren can read your thoughts," she called out, "you must try to believe what he has found there. We must all try. Trolls— think of trolls."

"Yes," Coren added. "Close your eyes and try to picture them. They are there, I promise you."

After a brief moment of hesitation, the little people did as he asked.

"All right." It was Coren's voice, but Lenora wasn't hearing it with her ears. It was inside her head. "Get ready," it was saying. "The little people are thinking about the trolls now. I'm going to gather up all their thoughts and throw them into your head. Then you have to will them into being."

Lenora wasn't altogether sure she liked him talking to her like that, but she nodded and then braced herself.

Coren turned back to the crowd. "Picture them. Concentrate hard."

Suddenly Lenora's head was full of a multitude of creatures, fuzzy-haired creatures with one head and two heads and three heads, and they were so cute, adorable, and she knew all their names and everything about them all at once! They were real! She wanted them to be real! They had to be real, just had to! Why, if they weren't real, she'd just close her eyes and scream until they became real. Then suddenly she felt a tremendous surge of energy and the air around her crackled and was filled with hideous roars and frightened screams.

It had worked. Every inch of space was covered in trolls!

19

There were, perhaps, thousands of trolls. They were about the same size as the little people, with shoulders twice as broad, flat faces, large noses, and eyes that glittered and bulged. Some had two heads, and some had more.

"We did it." Coren grinned, still shaking from the effort.

"Yes," Lenora agreed. "We certainly did."

The trolls were in a fit of terror and anxiety, not knowing where they were, what had happened, or what would happen.

The little people were also terrified. They ran into their little enclosures, grabbing their children, screaming in fear.

"They're ugly! They're filthy! They're horrible! Send them back."

"We have to do something!" Peetr called out, over the increasing din.

Lenora and Muni and the others nodded. They tried to shout over the roars and screams in an effort to get everyone to calm down. Coren just sank down to the ground and covered his face with his hands. Lenora looked at him and shook her head. He gave up so easily.

The trolls slowly began to quiet. It started with the children, who wandered over to Coren, looking at him with some curiosity, and it quickly spread to the adults. Lenora's and Muni's shouts of "Calm down, be quiet, stop shouting" soon dwindled away as they watched the crowd form around Coren.

He looked up and smiled.

"You don't have to be afraid," he said to the trolls. "This is real. We've brought you back."

So, Lenora realized, Coren hadn't given up. He had been communicating, mind to mind, with the trolls!

And with the little people too, it seemed—for now they began to edge out of the caves and approach the trolls. For a moment, nobody spoke. The two groups just stood there, eyeing one another in disbelief.

It was Sumra who broke the silence.

"Hulder?" she said as she gazed at a troll with two heads. "Is—is it you?"

"Yes," the troll's two heads said simultaneously. "It's us!" Hulder rushed over, embraced Sumra, and kissed her on both cheeks at the same time.

After that, it was pandemonium, as old friends recognized one another and rushed to meet again. All of the thoughts Hevak had planted about how disgusting the trolls were had disappeared like clouds after rain. Laughter and conversation filled the caves.

In the midst of it all, Coren motioned Lenora over. Muni and Lero followed her.

"What is it?" Lenora asked as he moved them slightly away from the jubilant crowd.

"When I went to touch the trolls' minds, to try to calm them," Coren answered, "I saw something. Something else!"

"What was it?" Muni demanded. Coren noted that she didn't seem to have any qualms about him reading the trolls' minds.

"I saw memories," he said, "just like your memories of the trolls. The trolls have things in their minds which your people have no memory of at all."

"Things?" said Muni, bewildered. "What are you talking about?"

"There are others who have been banished from this land," Coren said with growing certainty. "Hevak must have been sending groups off into the gray for years now. Throwing them out like so much garbage!"

"What—things—have you seen?" Lenora said.

"Elves! And fairies!"

Muni and Lero exchanged perplexed glances.

"I have not heard such names before," said Muni. "Elves? Fairies?"

"I've read about them," Lenora said.

"They're very cute and very little," Coren

explained, "much smaller than you, Muni. And the fairies can fly."

"Oh sure," Lero said. "And puppy dogs are blue!"

Lenora's mind was too busy to even hear him. "You know," she said thoughtfully to Muni and Lero, "the way the elves and fairies are to the trolls must be the way the trolls were to you. And just like you are right now to the big people. And," she continued, "if we can convince the trolls to bring back the elves and fairies, then all of us together should be able to defeat Hevak somehow. As I said before, the more the merrier!

"Exactly!" Coren agreed.

"I can't argue with that," Lero said. "But I'll believe it when I see it."

"Good," said Lenora. "The sooner you see it the better. Let's get to work."

They hurried back to the crowd, and Lero and Lenora shouted to get everyone's attention. But the trolls were just as reluctant to believe in elves and fairies as the little people had been to believe in the trolls. Given their own recent experience, however, it wasn't very hard for Lenora to convince them.

Or rather, Coren thought with some admiration, just bully them into it.

Soon the whole throng stood around Coren once again, trolls and little people together, eyes closed, all thinking about elves and fairies. As he went into their minds, he could feel the energy gathering, then building, building, building. The air crackled just as it did before a lightning strike.

"Now!" he yelled. Once more, Lenora's mind was filled with strange knowledge, and she made it true. The air was filled with wings, and the ground underfoot was covered with tiny scampering brown creatures.

The fairies flew about in a frenzy, many of them damaging their wings and falling to the ground. They were delicate creatures dressed in a gauzy material, their wings translucent. There were males, females, even children.

The elves were dressed in leather breeches, shirts, and boots. They were hollering, screaming, laughing with joy, doing somersaults, cartwheels, playing little flutes. They seemed to suffer none of the shock of return the others did, but immediately began festivities.

Lenora looked around. She smiled. They practically had an army now!

But how could they use it? Even with so many, what could they do against Hevak's mighty power? There were lots of them, true, but they had no weapons, and Hevak was so strong. If he had willed them all out of existence once . . . Oh yes, they had to be careful. They had to think it through, work out a plan.

Lenora's thoughts were interrupted as the hubbub

around her grew in strength. She looked out over the crowd to see little people and trolls and fairies all gesturing wildly as they shouted at one another. Surely, they weren't all getting angry at one another again?

"Hevak did this," she heard a little person tell a troll nearby. "We praised him, and then he just threw us away, like smelly old garbage. No offense intended."

"None taken," the troll said, and then nodded as he listened to a fairy hovering and trilling into his hairy right ear. "You're right, if this is true, we shouldn't stand for it. We should do something!"

"We should give him a piece of our minds," said an elf as she jumped lightly onto the troll's broad shoulders and did a handstand there. "A taste of his own medicine!"

Similar conversations were taking place all over, and before Lenora realized it, the entire crowd was chanting in unison, their fists waving in the air. "Get Hevak! Get Hevak! Get Hevak!"

Their army was turning into a hysterical mob! Everything would be ruined! Lenora turned to Peetr and Lero for help, but they weren't there anymore, nor, for that matter, were Muni and Sumra. She gazed anxiously into the crowd and finally, caught sight of them. They too had venomous looks on their faces and were waving fists in the air as they chanted along with the rest. "Get Hevak! Get Hevak!"

In the midst of the growing tumult, Lenora saw

Coren standing, eyes closed, forehead wrinkled in concentration. He must be trying to calm them again. Oh, please, Lenora thought, let it work. It's our only chance.

She stood there helplessly, silently urging Coren on. Suddenly his face went white. He slumped and fell to the ground. "Coren!" she cried. As she pushed her way toward him, the mob abruptly surged forward, nearly trampling both her and Coren in the rush to get up to the corridor and out of the cave.

Before long, Lenora sat alone in the middle of a mammoth empty space, cradling the unconscious Coren's head in her lap and listening to the chant fading in the distance. "Get Hevak! Get Hevak!"

20

Coren groaned. His eyes opened, and he looked up at Lenora in bewilderment.

"I tried," he said, his voice groggy. "But I couldn't do it. They were like one powerful mind. It was just too strong for me."

"Well, you tried at least. But now what are we going to do? Rushing off like that without any plan— how could they? Hevak will just blot them all right out of existence again. They've ruined everything!"

"You're right," Coren said urgently. "We've got to catch up with them and stop them. It's our only chance!" As he struggled to get up on his feet, he groaned again and nearly fell.

"Perhaps I should stay here," he said miserably. "In this condition, I'll just slow you down."

But Lenora wasn't having any of it. "No!" she said. "You're coming if I have to carry you! I need you."

Coren looked up at her, astonished. She needed him?

"You do?"

"Of course I do," she said impatiently. "How else

can I know what everybody is thinking?"

"Oh," he said, gingerly taking a step. Of course—it was the powers she needed.

"It makes me so angry," she continued. "If my powers weren't blocked I could fix this mess in a minute! You know what I'd do? I'd create my own army! One that didn't just panic all of a sudden! With machines and thousands of fighting men—and women, I don't see why women can't fight—and maybe even monsters, scary monsters, spidery monsters with tentacles! No one could defeat us, no one!" She shrugged. "But it seems that without you I'm as helpless as a two-year-old."

"You are never helpless, Lenora," Coren stated emphatically, not as a compliment, just as a simple fact. And she confirmed it by grabbing his hand and pulling him up the rocky slope toward the corridor.

It was not a happy trip. Lenora pulled a stumbling Coren along behind her, ignoring his requests to slow down. Meanwhile, Coren ignored Lenora's constant orders to stop whining and get a move on. By the time they reached the upper levels, they were both out of breath and very irritated with one another.

At last, the walls of the corridor began to be interrupted by doors—they were near the top, and the city was just above their heads. Lenora dropped Coren's hand and let him slump to the ground. "So?" she said.

"So what?" he snapped back.

"You know! What are they thinking? What are

they doing? Which door do we go through?"

"Oh. Right." Coren had been so busy keeping himself on his feet and complaining that he hadn't tuned in on the thoughts above.

As Lenora watched anxiously, his face changed. He broke into a huge smile. "Well!" he exclaimed.

"What?" she said impatiently. "What is it?"

"Let's go up and you'll see," he said. He pulled himself to his feet and rushed down the corridor toward one of the doors, Lenora at his heels.

The scene that confronted them was curious indeed. It was the same huge square they had come to when they had first arrived in Farren, and it was filled with people, just as it had been then. This time, however, the Gragians were not alone. Everywhere there were trolls, elves, little people, fairies—and all of them were very, very busy.

Some fairies buzzed around the heads of Gragians and pinched them. Other fairies flew down inside the Gragians' clothing—and they must have been tickling them in tender places, because those Gragians were laughing uncontrollably.

Some little people were undoing the Gragians' garments, while others just walked up to the Gragians and boxed them on their ears. Still other little people danced around gleefully, grabbing baskets of food from the Gragians and promptly tossing various fruits and vegetables at their heads.

Trolls were running at the Gragians and bowling them over, or kneeling down in front of them and chortling as the Gragians stumbled into them and fell.

And elves—elves were everywhere, taking hats from some Gragians and dropping them on the heads of others, tying their shoelaces together, or dumping pots of water over them.

Laughter filled the air: grisly troll chortles, elf hoots, fairy giggles.

In the midst of all this, the citizens of Farren City stood, or fell, their shoelaces tied together, their clothes covered with food or dripping with water, their pants a tangled mess. But the weirdest thing was, their eyes were filled with horror, and they did nothing to stop the strange attacks.

"I don't understand," said Lenora.

"Hevak's people can't see our people," Coren crowed. "That's the one thing we forgot!"

At that moment, Lero and Muni rushed up to them out of the crowd.

"It's about time you two got here," Lero said. "What took you so long?"

"Isn't it wonderful," Muni said, her eyes glowing. "I've wanted to do this for years, but I never had the courage!"

"Never had the numbers, you mean," said Lero, equally excited. "We never could have done all this by ourselves! Look! They don't know what's happening to them, and it's driving them crazy!"

"Or, maybe," Coren said enthusiastically, "driving them sane!"

"What?" said Lenora. "What do you mean?"

"I mean, the block Hevak put in their minds is starting to crumble! I can feel it going! With all this happening at once, Hevak is losing control of them!"

As Lenora watched, Coren's words came true before her eyes. A woman suddenly blinked and then looked right into the eyes of the elf who was standing on the shoulders of a troll and tickling her nose with a feather.

"Agh," she screamed. "Monsters! The world is full of monsters!"

Similar shrieks came from all directions.

"Hevak isn't going to have any time to worry about us now," Coren said. "He'll have to divert his energies to his people, to stop them from remembering, to stop them from seeing everyone. Even Hevak can't do everything at once!"

Lenora watched the Gragians scream and flee in terror, pursued by their army of tormentors. Coren was right—this chaos might be just what they needed.

She turned toward Coren to tell him so—and then stopped. His eyes were full of fear.

21

Coren felt the buzzing inside his mind only seconds before he heard it with his ears. It was coming from above, and he knew what it was. Flying transports.

Like silver darts piercing the skies above him, they cruised into view. And along with them came the thoughts of the guards controlling them. They were thoughts of death, doom, and destruction. They were preparing to drop some horrible weapon on the square.

"What is it?" Lenora asked anxiously.

"Flying machines!" he told her. "Look—up there!"

Lero followed Coren's and Lenora's gaze into the sky. "I know what to do about that," he said. "Leave it to me!"

He leaped to his feet and ran back toward a group of fairies that were hovering over a poor little Gragian child, tickling him all over. "Hey, you!" he shouted. "Over here!"

The fairies flew to meet him and, after a short buzz of conversation, zoomed up into the sky. Coren and Lenora watched anxiously as the fairies moved toward the flying machines. Soon the machines began to twist and turn erratically and plunge dangerously low over the crowd. Then they swooped upward again, nearly hitting the tall buildings, and then lurched back toward the palace and out of sight.

Lero returned, chuckling. "It must be odd to have all your instruments and controls suddenly develop a life of their own!"

"Good work, Lero," Muni said.

"But everything won't be that easy," Lenora said grimly. "Who knows what other nasty tricks Hevak has up his sleeve."

As the Gragians became more conscious of their enemies, they desperately tried to fight them off. It was turning into a pitched battle. As Lenora watched, an infuriated Gragian grabbed a gossamer-winged fairy who hovered in front of him and slammed her down over poor old Peetr's head, knocking both Peetr and the fairy unconscious.

"That's my father, you oversized bully," Muni screamed. And she and Lero rushed off in pursuit of the Gragian.

Suddenly a loud noise filled the air. It came from Hevak's palace at the far end of the square. As Lenora turned toward the sound, the main doors of the palace flew open, and two rows of trumpeters, clad in red and white, marched out and took up positions on either side of the doorway. They continued to play as row upon row of guards followed them—all bearing weapons, all looking fierce and determined. The guards poured out of the palace in a seemingly endless stream and divided into two columns, one moving left and one moving right as they took up positions around the edges of the crowd.

"We have to do something," Lenora said urgently. "Fast!"

But the entire square was surrounded by guards. They came to a halt, turned to face inward toward the crowd, and simultaneously, as if controlled by one mind, raised their threatening-looking weapons to their shoulders. The crowd was so intent on its battle that it hardly even noticed them.

The trumpets blared even louder, and through the door of the palace came a strange object, a kind of barge or sled that floated in midair with no visible means of support. One figure stood on it, clad in white. It was Hevak.

He stood firmly in place, not even swaying as his transport skimmed over the turmoil below and came to a stop hovering a few feet in front of where Lenora stood beside a trembling Coren. With one final blast, the trumpets grew silent.

Hevak stood there like a statue, ignoring the fighting and screaming, his eyes glowering as he stared down from his high perch at Lenora.

"It's you," he said finally. "I might have known it

would be you. And," he added distastefully, "you've brought along all the misfits I rejected from my perfect world. Well, I'm sorry, my dear, but I don't want them back here!"

Suddenly all the little people and trolls and elves and fairies began to flicker. One moment, they were busily punching and prodding and sticking their fingers in the Gragians' eyes. The next moment, they seemed to shimmer and began to disappear.

How dare he? I don't want them to disappear, Lenora told herself. And in an instant, they were back.

"Go away!" Hevak blazed, his glance darting this way and that at the intruders in the square. "I command you to go away!"

Once more they blinked out.

And, once more, they returned.

"Lenora," Coren shouted. "You did it! With all these distractions, he can't block your powers!"

"I won't have it!" Hevak shrieked. "I don't want them."

"Well, I do," Lenora said, staring up calmly into his face.

The wave of hostility that poured from Hevak struck Coren's mind like a blast from a furnace.

"I can see," Hevak said, glaring at Lenora, "that I'm going to have to deal with you first." Then he threw his arms into the air in a dramatic gesture.

"Let there be—monsters!" he shouted.

And there were, in the air over their heads—hundreds of them. They were spiders, giant spiders with massive bodies, wide cavernous mouths filled with sharp teeth, bulging red-veined eyes, and long slimy green tentacles. They were perched on a massive web that now hung between the spires of the tall buildings around the square, and they immediately began to descend from the web on slimy tendrils. Everyone in the square below screamed in terror.

Including Lenora. These were creatures from her very worst nightmares. She started to shiver.

"You can do it, Lenora," an urgent voice said inside her head. It was Coren. "You can get rid of those things. I know you can! You know you can—you just have to believe they're not there! Do it. And do it fast, before they land on us!"

But Lenora was finding it hard to believe that those awful monsters weren't there. One of them hovered directly over her head and reached down a slimy feeler.

It touched her. It burned like acid.

No, it didn't—because she didn't want it to. She gathered all her strength and focused it on the monster over her head.

At first nothing happened. Then the tentacle touching her disappeared. Then the body, leaving only the sharp teeth and jaws hovering in the air above her. Encouraged, Lenora thought even harder. With one large angry bellow, every single one of the spiders winked out of existence.

She sighed with relief.

Coren threw his arms around her and hugged her. "That was wonderful!" he exclaimed. "I knew you could do it, I knew it!"

She grinned and felt so happy that she couldn't stop herself. She hugged him back, and then went one step further and kissed him.

When she opened her eyes and saw the giddy look on his face she laughed, but the laugh was cut short.

"Enough childish games," Hevak said. "It's time to get serious."

Up went his arms again, and the troops around the square no longer wore red. Instead, their uniforms were white, furry white. They began to grow, getting larger and larger until they became massive white bears. They flashed their sharp claws as they butted their way through the terrified crowd and lumbered toward Lenora.

I would have been frightened of those, once, she thought. But now? They hardly even made her shiver. She fixed her eyes on the closest bear and watched scornfully as it did as she demanded and turned into a cute pink puppy. It looked up at her and whimpered, then fled and ran, followed by a barking herd of puppies of all colors.

Hevak watched their wagging tails as they loped off

through the crowd toward the nearest exit, then turned and looked down at Lenora with eyes of ice.

"That does it," he said. "You've pushed me too far." His transport suddenly rose straight up into the air until he stood high above the crowd. "Ready!" he shouted, and there was an audible click as the guards surrounding the square prepared their weapons. "Aim!" he added, and finally, "Fire!"

Thousands of tiny but lethal projectiles whizzed through the air toward Lenora—and toward Coren!

"No!" She raised her hand, and the projectiles suddenly stopped in midair. Then, in a weird ballet, they danced toward and around one another, and as Coren and the others watched in amazement, flew upward and joined together to become an anvil—a huge iron anvil, suspended directly over Hevak's head and plummeting fast.

That's some wicked imagination she's got, Coren thought. I'm glad she's on my side.

Even from far below, they could see Hevak's eyes blaze fury toward the descending anvil until, just a few inches above his head, it exploded. Pieces of it flew everywhere.

A fire storm formed in the air above them, above the entire square, including the guards. Hevak was so angry that he no longer cared who got hurt.

Lenora concentrated all her energy. The heat was intense, becoming fiercer and fiercer. Everyone was screaming in fear. Flames began to lick at the heads of the taller Gragians. Horrible screams of pain and the smell of burned hair and clothes filled the air. Quickly, Lenora produced a light rain. The drizzle turned into a downpour. Thunder roared. Lightning cracked. The fires went out.

Everyone in the square stood silent, too amazed to say or do anything, as water dripped from their clothes and their hair.

"And my suit was finally dry," Coren said to Lenora, a rueful smile on his face.

22

Hevak's transport descended right to the ground. He stepped off and moved toward them through the puddles with a purposeful stride. Coren quickly placed himself in front of Lenora. Lenora couldn't help but appreciate his instinct to protect her. Still, gently, she pushed him aside and tried to face Hevak without flinching.

The look on Hevak's face surprised her. Anger had been replaced by his dazzling smile.

"Impressive, that storm," he said. "Nimble work. It proves I was right in the first place. You belong here in Grag, with me."

"That's not what you said when you threw me into prison!" Lenora snapped. "And those spiders, that fire—if you want me here, you certainly have a strange way of showing it."

"I'm sorry, my dear. I truly am. Surely you realize what a nuisance you've been? But that's just the point. Now that I've seen what you can do—well, it would be foolish of me to send you away, most foolish indeed.

You belong here, my dear. You'll realize I'm right, once you understand."

"Understand? Understand what?"

Hevak flashed his white teeth. "Let me show you."

Coren reached out from behind Lenora and put a hand on her arm. "Be careful," he whispered.

"Shut up," Hevak lashed out at him, "or you're gone."

"You just leave Coren alone, you big bully," she said angrily, but as she glared at him, his eyes caught hers, and something happened.

She was him. She was Hevak. For some reason, he was making her think his thoughts, experience what he experienced.

"Lenora," Coren hissed inside her mind. "It's dangerous! Close your mind. Don't let him in."

But Lenora couldn't hear him. She was Hevak. Hevak the Great, Hevak the Magnificent. He stood in front of a cheering throng, luxuriating in pride as they called out his name.

I deserve this praise, he said to himself. Next to me they are like tiny insects, powerless, meaningless nothings.

And then a shadow of doubt crossed his mind.

Too meaningless, too powerless. They bend to my will with ease, even though secretly they hate me, try to resist me. I'm too strong for them. They're no challenge anymore. I need a challenge, a new challenge. I need new worlds to conquer. I'll send a message through space, through time! I'll find those of strong mind, the discontented ones, and I'll send them a vision they can't resist. And then I'll bend them to my will. Soon all the universes will be mine!

Ah, Lenora thought as Hevak's memories filled her mind. So that's it—that's why I had that vision, why I came here. How could he be so arrogant?

There was more. Now Hevak was guiding her deeper into his mind, down into an earlier layer of memories. He was observing himself in a mirror, admiring his shiny dark hair, his brilliant blue eyes, his strong manly jaw. And as he gazed into the mirror, he was thinking about the little people.

They are repulsive, he thought, puny. How could I have ever thought otherwise? It's upsetting for my people even to look at them. The whole country would be better off if the ugly little things couldn't be seen at all. As the saying goes, out of sight, out of mind.

Hevak is despicable, Lenora thought.

Hevak seemed to sense her repulsion. Flooding into her head came more memories, preventing her from thinking her own thoughts.

Once again Hevak was looking at his face in the mirror. It was a different face now, younger, softer. Much softer—almost feminine.

It was feminine, Lenora realized with a jolt.

Hevak was a woman.

I'm tired of being female, Hevak was saying to herself. They all claim to respect me, these people of mine, but they don't really. They'd treat me differently if I were a man. Men always get more respect. I'll do it. I'll transform myself.

Again Lenora hurtled backward into the past, down through the layers of Hevak's memory, catching myriads of images of Hevak's life as a woman and a queen—choosing her wardrobe, governing her people, ordering her meals. Lenora caught images of little people mixed in with larger ones at a time when the little people had strolled Hevak's land as equals.

Equals at least to everyone but Hevak—not to Hevak. Always she was taking, getting, being the center of attention. And always, she was unhappy, dissatisfied, wanting more.

And now Lenora was descending down again, deeper, deeper into Hevak's memory. Hevak was observing herself in a mirror. Had she spent her whole life looking in mirrors? She was younger now, only a few years older than Lenora herself. She looked strangely familiar. Who—? But her head was filled once more with Hevak's thoughts.

This world I've made isn't good enough, Hevak was telling herself. I haven't succeeded. It's full of ugly things and ugly people. Oh, naturally, they all look up to me and praise me. Why shouldn't they? I created them, after all; but everywhere I go I see flaws, I'm reminded of imperfection. It's just not good enough.

I'll change it all, she decided. I'll make everyone perfect! The women will all be beautiful! The men will all be handsome! There will be no ugly trolls, no nasty little elves or fairies!

And then again Lenora was sliding down into the depths of Hevak's memories. Hevak was looking at her own reflection once more.

This time, it wasn't in a mirror. The reflection rippled. It must be a pool. Behind Hevak was a shadowy presence, a fuzzy image of a pale face, of red hair. And Hevak herself, Hevak was—

It can't be! thought Lenora. It can't!

But it was. It was her own face.

This younger Hevak was—herself!

23

As Lenora watched, she saw image after image from Hevak's early past. Hevak being chased down a stairway by puppies of many different colors, then being rescued by a tall dark knight, a knight who looked exactly like Hevak himself did now. Hevak cheerfully gathering herbs in the woods with Lufa. Hevak trying out various worlds of her own creations and being punished for it. A child Hevak making the chairs talk, playing fantasy games with a beautiful doll with blond hair piled on its head; an even younger Hevak trying to fly down a staircase and hurting herself.

These are mine! thought Lenora. Mine! My memories! Not his!

Suddenly, her mind cleared. She felt very unsteady, but Coren held her up.

"What does this mean?" she said to Hevak, her voice shaky.

"It means what you think it does, Lenora. I am you. You created all this. You imagined this world, and you imagined yourself in it. You jumped into it, many years ago. And you exercised your powers, you became stronger and stronger. You became me, Hevak. When I sent a message out for new people, I never imagined it would be powerful enough to go into the past as well as the present. I never imagined I would catch myself! Such strength, such amazing, wonderful power!" And he suddenly laughed out loud, a mancal laugh.

Then he took her hand in his. "You want to join me, Lenora, my dear, myself. I know you do. I know you can't resist. You want to feel that power. Rule a land. Rule with me."

So many things were running through Lenora's mind that she could barely think. Had all this really developed out of one of her imaginings? If so, then she supposed Hevak was her.

And yet she knew that no matter what he said, he wasn't her. She could never have purposefully made the trolls and elves and fairies disappear. She could never treat the little people so badly or send Coren off into the gray. Could she?

"No!" she cried. "I refuse to become you! I won't allow it to happen!"

And she pictured him disappearing, first his legs, then his arms, then his body, and finally, his head, the laugh still on his lips.

"You stupid child!" he cried. "Do you really think you can defeat me, now that my powers have grown so?" Then, enticingly, he added, "Do you really think you want to defeat me?"

She did—didn't she?

For a moment she hesitated, uncertain.

"Don't give in to him," Coren said. "I'm here with you, Lenora. We'll defeat him together."

"Do you choose that?" Hevak sneered at Lenora. "Do you choose that over me?"

In the minds of both Coren and Lenora an image appeared, a picture of a skinny, hunched-over, middle-aged man, his face pinched. A freckled fussbudget with a few strands of red hair around a shiny bald pate, frightened of everything, sitting alone in a dusty room, and wondering if it was safe to eat nectarines so early in the season.

"That's him, my dear," Hevak snarled. "The real him as he'll someday be."

Lenora hesitated for only the briefest of instants. She remembered Coren standing in front of her, trying to protect her even though he knew he didn't have the strength.

"That's not Coren," she screamed at Hevak, "and I'm not you!"

Hevak's face twisted in fury. "Then your doom is sealed," he hissed.

There was a pain in her head, a terrible pain, so intense she could hardly remember who she was or what was happening.

This is it, she thought, he's sending me into the gray. I'm going, I'm—

But Coren was speaking again. "Lenora, if Hevak was you once, then you are as strong as he is, and you can defeat him."

He was right. Suddenly, with him saying it, she knew she could. She felt stronger. Power surged through her and from her, like a bolt of lightning—and she directed it straight at Hevak, willing him not to be.

For a moment, nothing happened. Hevak stood his ground, but then, abruptly, his eyes took on a look of horror. His face contorted, wavered, then reformed again, a younger version. And then that face changed too, became more feminine.

Hevak's life spun backward, unwinding before their very eyes. All the images of himself that Hevak had shown to Lenora in her mind rapidly succeeded one another as the Hevak standing before them grew younger and younger. Finally, only one image remained.

Lenora stood transfixed: It was like looking into a mirror. Hevak floated resplendent, her mother's white wedding gown gleaming, the gold hair ribbon sparkling, her arms outstretched.

"Lenora," a plaintive voice called from that perfect image of her own mouth. "We are one. We are great. We are strong. Oh, Lenora—you know what you really want. Join me. Join me."

For a moment Lenora's resolve weakened. How could she kill herself? But it wasn't her. It was no more her than the image of herself she saw in the mirror. It wasn't her at all.

She reached for Coren in her mind and he was there, calming her, helping her focus. Then, in a final burst of energy, their powers working together, they threw Hevak away.

With a last cry of rage, Hevak began to spin, faster and faster, becoming a child and then an infant, until the image whirled into nothingness. Hevak was no more.

In the same moment, Lenora felt herself fall. The power that had filled her seeped away and she felt too weak to even breathe. Blackness swam around her and she knew nothing.

24

The first thing Lenora was aware of was Coren's presence. Even though her eyes were closed, she could feel someone holding her hand and she knew it was him. But she was too tired to look, and she let the black claim her once more.

Again she swam out of the darkness, and again she was aware of Coren. May as well find out, she thought as she slowly opened her eyes, whether I'm dead or alive.

Coren sat looking down at her, and by his side was Muni.

No, it wasn't Muni. It was Lufa. Funny how alike those two looked, but this was definitely Lufa.

That wasn't possible. How could Lufa be here? Where had she come from? Where were Muni and the rest? Were they all dead? Or had she merely lost her mind?

Lufa took her hand.

"You're in Gepeth. You're back home. And you'll soon be well. Drink this."

Lufa raised Lenora's head and poured a sip of strong

liquid down her throat, reminding her of Muni and another awakening. Then, gently, Lufa placed Lenora's head back down on the pillow. Lenora closed her eyes. She was so tired. She drifted away.

The next time she awoke there was no one hovering over her. There was nothing but darkness. Had it been a dream then, Lufa and Coren caring for her? It must have been. This was reality. Hevak had won and she was alone, in the dark.

But that certainly isn't what Lufa had taught her to expect when she died. Where was the bright light, her ancestors—?

And if Hevak had made her disappear, shouldn't it be gray, not black?

She tried to call Coren's name but couldn't. She was too weak for her voice to obey her wishes.

"Lenora?" It was Coren.

Crash.

"Blast. Ouch. Don't worry, Lenora, I'm here. You're all right."

She felt his hand on hers.

"Tripped over something in the dark."

Poor lad, so clumsy. She gave his hand a little squeeze.

"I'm sorry," he continued. "I fell asleep, but I thought I heard you call."

Call? But she hadn't—was he reading her mind again? She'd have to speak to him about that! As soon as she found the strength to open her mouth.

A light sprang up across the room, and then Lufa was standing over her too, a candle illuminating her and Coren.

"How are you, Lenora dear?" Lufa asked. "Had quite an adventure, I understand."

Lenora just gazed at Lufa's smiling face, then at Coren.

"You aren't dreaming," Coren reassured her. "Don't worry. Go to sleep. In the morning we'll explain everything." And then, as if in answer to her request, "I'll stay here by your bed. Just sleep now."

Lenora sighed and felt a tear trickle down her cheek. She didn't know why. She shut her eyes and went to sleep.

This time, bright light woke her. She opened her eyes and realized immediately that she was in Lufa's cottage. The morning light was streaming through one of the large windows. She was home!

"But how?" she exclaimed. She could speak again!

Coren was asleep in a chair beside her bed, holding her hand. He awoke with a start. She stared at her hand, clasped tightly in his. He followed her gaze, then quickly dropped her hand, his face coloring. It was nice, the way he always did that.

Lufa entered and waved Coren away, then sat Lenora up and held a goblet to her lips. She drank more of the strong liquid, then fell back on the pillow.

"I'm not dreaming?" Lenora said. "How do I know that for sure?"

"Well," Lufa smiled, "I suppose none of us really knows that. Perhaps this is all a dream, a fantasy we will wake out of."

Lenora started at Lufa's mild joke. According to Hevak, his world was her fantasy—come to think of it, that was probably why Muni looked so much like Lufa. And if her imaginings could be real, then who was to say that her reality wasn't somebody else's dream?

Panicking, she grabbed Lufa's arm. It felt warm, solid, real. Surely something this solid couldn't be just a figment of somebody's imagination. Could it?

Seeing the anxiety on Lenora's face, Lufa squeezed her hand and hastened to reassure her. "Don't worry, my dear. There's nothing to worry about. It's not a dream. For now, Lenora, this is reality, yours and mine—the reality you grew up in, the reality you escaped from, and now, thank heavens, the reality you've returned to."

But that didn't mean it was any more real than any other reality, did it? Or any less of a dream.

And now, even Hevak seemed like part of a dream. That last moment—

"But what happened?" Lenora asked, dropping Lufa's hand and turning her eyes to Coren, who was still hovering anxiously near the bed, just out of Lufa's view. "The last thing I remember was this blast of power, and you and I were together, and—and—"

Coren moved toward the bed again, smiling. "We defeated Hevak. Demolished him! And then there was quite an uproar. The Gragians who hadn't been sent into the gray had to adjust to all the Gragians who had just reappeared. It looked like it was going to get very interesting." He paused. "I must say that I was worried about them all, I mean after we got rid of Hevak and you collapsed. I wondered if everyone in that world would just disappear without at least one of you around to will them to exist."

"But they didn't?" Lenora asked anxiously.

"No. It seems that, once created, they have a life of their own."

"I'm so glad." Then a thought occurred to her. "Good heavens, Coren, does this mean that all the other places I've imagined still exist too? Have they all got a life of their own?"

Coren and Lufa exchanged glances.

"Coren and I have been discussing just that," Lufa said. "We aren't sure, but well, I think it's possible."

For a long moment they were all silent as the implications of it sank in. All those worlds . . . Then Lufa tried to hide the worried look on her face by propping up a pillow and helping Lenora to sit up in bed.

"But how did we get back here?" Lenora asked.

"Oh." Coren shrugged. "That was easy. I just used my power. I contacted my parents, mind to mind. And then your parents and my parents got together, and they formed a group and literally pulled us back here to Gepeth!"

"And when I saw you like that," Lufa said, "I told them all to go away and leave you to me. You need rest and quiet. I finally got them to agree, even that willful old bear of a father of yours! They brought you here to my house, and here you've been ever since." Lufa leaned over and gave her a careful look, then nodded. "And it's done wonders, too. Or else"—she turned to glance briefly at Coren—"something has done wonders. I think we might even be able to get a little food into you."

Lenora suddenly realized that she was absolutely ravenous. Of course she was, she'd really eaten nothing since that gala dinner at Hevak's palace.

"Yes," she said. "Please! I'm starved. Bacon, I think, and scrambled eggs and pancakes. And a big bowl of roast-flavored oatmeal!"

"No," Lufa said. "A light meal to start with. Too much food at once would only make you feel sick. Roast-flavored oatmeal indeed! I'll go prepare some broth with herbs." She turned to Coren. "You stay here and keep her company, young man," she ordered as she left the room.

"It's been three days," Coren told Lenora after Lufa left. "I was so worried."

He smiled down at her. She smiled back.

For a moment, they were both at a loss for words.

"Well," Lenora said.

"Well," Coren repeated.

Suddenly something occurred to Lenora. "All those people Hevak sent back to their own countries, will they become little dictators, too, do you think? Are they still trying to make their lands ready for Hevak, right this very minute?"

"That's an interesting thought," Coren replied. "Maybe they are." Then he noticed the stricken look on her face. "But without Hevak's power behind them," he continued, "surely they're bound to fail. And who knows, maybe their desire to follow Hevak's vision died with him?"

"I hope you're right," Lenora sighed.

"That might help, too," he said. "You hoping it, I mean."

Lenora definitely did not like to be reminded of the bizarre connection between herself and Hevak. She cast through her mind to find a safer topic.

"Coren," she finally said, "do you remember those weird creatures that arrived, there on the hill with all the others?"

Coren nodded. "I do. Poor old Hevak—when he called for the best, he didn't get what he expected, did he?"

"It served him right! Narrow-minded old fool! But what I'm wondering is, do you think he made all those creatures disappear? Like the trolls and the others, I mean? Did he send them into that gray place?"

"Oh, no, no, I don't think so. Why bother? He probably just cut off the call and sent them all right back home again."

"Then at least we know their worlds are safe," Lenora said. "Oh, how could Hevak be so mean? How could I—" She stopped in midsentence and turned away from Coren, filled with distress. Because there was no avoiding it. Hevak had started out as her. She had created that whole miserable place. "I suppose it means that I don't dare ever imagine anything else," she wailed. "I can't live without imagining things, Coren, I just can't!"

Coren took her hand. "But why should you live without it?" he said. "That place—well, it had its flaws, I suppose—but was it really all that bad?"

She looked at him in astonishment. "What do you mean?"

"I hate to admit it, Lenora, but there was a lot going on there I really liked. You can't give up imagining altogether just because things went a little wrong."

"A little wrong?"

"So fine, more than a little. But still, everyone there in Grag—the little people, the trolls—I bet if you asked them they wouldn't be sorry you imagined them there. They like their world. They even like one another. Remember Sumra and that two-headed troll, Hulder?

They were best friends, until Hevak interfered."

"But that's just it, Coren. Hevak did interfere."

"But suppose he didn't? I mean, if you were to imagine Grag now, wouldn't you do it differently?"

"Of course I would." She stared at him. "But I wish I didn't have to think about it at all! You're lucky," she muttered. "You don't have to worry that anything you imagine will become real."

Coren looked at her and shook his head. "You're wrong, you know," he said.

Lenora's eyebrows shot up. "Wrong?"

"Yes," he reiterated. "I mean, it's true I don't have your power—few people do. But everyone can still make what they imagine come true. Sometimes that's good—sometimes it isn't. And, well, you wouldn't be you if you didn't imagine things the way you do."

He seemed to be actually admiring her for it. "Do you mean," she teased, "that you liked our adventure? That you found it exciting?"

With some surprise, Coren realized that maybe he had. Now that it was all over, he could even look back on it with pleasure, sort of. It had been exciting. It had also been very alarming.

"Yes," he said, "if you can call almost disappearing forever or being eaten by giant spiders exciting, then, yes, it was! Much too exciting. Personally, I'd rather go for a leisurely stroll in the forest, and smell the flowers, and watch the birds."

"I like that too, of course," Lenora said. "But not as a steady diet. And," she added, "you don't want to end up like that picture of you Hevak showed us."

His response surprised her. "Maybe that would have been me, if I hadn't met you, Lenora."

Now it was her turn to blush.

"You drew me into your thoughts right from the start," he continued. "You remembered me when Hevak made everyone else forget about me. There must be a reason for that."

"Do you mean . . . ?" Lenora was too embarrassed to say it. She stared at him, and at this moment, strangely, he looked really handsome to her, far more so than those guards with their perfect good looks. His eyes were so compelling, in fact, that she had to look away.

"You do have some good qualities," she muttered, not wanting to let him know exactly how she felt.

"I do?" he said, truly surprised—he was using all his strength to stop himself from hearing her thoughts about him.

"Of course you do," she said angrily. "You're very reliable!"

"Boring, you mean."

"And logical."

"Yes," said Coren, grimacing, "that's true."

"And," Lenora leaned over and whispered in his ear, "you're a very good kisser!"

For a moment, Coren just looked at her. Then he

took her face in his hands and kissed her. It was as much a surprise to himself as it was to her.

"Well," Lufa said as she walked into the room carrying a steaming bowl of broth on a tray. "Does this mean wedding bells?"

Wedding bells? Marriage, to one another? Coren and Lenora both turned toward Lufa at once, panic in their eyes. Then they turned back and their eyes locked.

"We're not sure," Lenora said, staring into Coren's eyes.

"That's right," Coren agreed, staring right back. "We're not."

"Our parents will just have to wait," Lenora added.

"Yes, they will," Coren echoed. "They'll just have to wait."

For a moment neither spoke. They just kept looking at each other. And then, right in front of Lufa, they kissed again.

ABOUT THE AUTHORS

CAROL MATAS and PERRY NODELMAN are the co-authors of *Of Two Minds* and *More Minds*, a sequel to *Of Two Minds*, to be published by Point Fantasy in the summer of 1998.

CAROL MATAS has written numerous books for children and young adults, including *Lisa's War*, *Daniel's Story*, and *Sworn Enemies*. *Lisa's War* was listed as a Notable Book of the Year in the *New York Times Book Review* and as a Young Adults' Choice by the International Reading Association. Matas lives in Winnipeg, Canada, with her husband and two children.

PERRY NODELMAN is the author of *The Same Place but Different*. Nodelman lives in Winnipeg, Canada, with his wife and three children. He teaches English at the University of Winnipeg.

Fantastic Journeys to Other Worlds...

POINT FANTASY

☐ BCP45759-4	**Princess Nevermore** Dian Curtis Regan	$4.50
☐ BCP45896-5	**Shadow of the Red Moon** Walter Dean Myers	$4.50
☐ BCP97218-9	**Book of Enchantments** Patricia C. Wrede	$4.50
☐ BCP45722-5	**Enchanted Forest Chronicles, Book One:** **Dealing with Dragons** Patricia C. Wrede	$4.50
☐ BCP45721-7	**Enchanted Forest Chronicles, Book Two:** **Searching for Dragons** Patricia C. Wrede	$4.50
☐ BCP48467-2	**Enchanted Forest Chronicles, Book Three:** **Calling on Dragons** Patricia C. Wrede	$4.50
☐ BCP48475-3	**Enchanted Forest Chronicles, Book Four:** **Talking to Dragons** Patricia C. Wrede	$4.50